THE FUTURE UNDER PRESIDENT REAGAN

THE FUTURE UNDER PRESIDENT REAGAN

Edited by
WAYNE VALIS

With an Introduction by
ARAM BAKSHIAN JR.

ARLINGTON HOUSE PUBLISHERS
Westport, Connecticut

FOR JUNE AND HAROLD

Arlington House Publishers
333 Post Road West
Westport, Connecticut

Library of Congress Cataloging in Publication Data

The Future Under President Reagan.

1 United States Politics and Government 1981, Addresses, essays, lectures.   2. United States— Economic policy —1971-   —Addresses, essays, lectures.   3. United States — social conditions — 1960-   —Addresses, essays, lectures.   4. Reagan, Ronald — Addresses, essays, lectures.   I. Valis, Wayne.
E876.F87   973927   80-29277
ISBN 0-87000-504-9

Manufactured in the United States of America

9 8 7 6 5 4 3 2 1

CONTENTS

PREFACE

Where will Ronald Reagan lead America during his first term in office? How will he deal with urgent domestic and foreign policies? What kind of man is Ronald Reagan? And how will he perform as President? Pressing questions in these times. In response this book will examine various aspects of his personal life, character and personality, his career, and the policies and programs he can be expected to propose and support.

No attempt was made to produce an encyclopedic or all-inclusive volume, nor is this a scholarly work. Many public policy issues are discussed briefly — or not at all. The choice of topics was mine alone. Issues selected for consideration reflect my own best judgment about those that will be emphasized during the first years of the Reagan Presidency. They were central issues in the campaign, and they are the issues on which President Reagan's success or failure, reelection or defeat, will rest. If he is to succeed in realigning American politics, he will do so only by crystallizing public support around his approaches to these broad issues.

The Future Under President Reagan was written by scholars and political practitioners familiar with Ronald Reagan, his record in California, his ideas, programs, and policies. Many contributors have played key roles in Reagan's California governorship or in his campaign for the Presidency. Some will hold positions of trust in a Reagan Administration, and all share a strong support for the new President. Although not neutral about Reagan, the contributors have attempted to assess objectively the difficulties and limitations that will confront the Reagan Presidency and have devoted special efforts to predict the probable course of the first years of his term in office. It is hoped that this volume will aid in a better and more informed public understanding of the new President and his philosophy of government. Ideas and recommendations in these pages will also contribute, we hope, to the coming public policy debate.

The views expressed and the conclusions reached in this book are entirely personal and are those of the individual authors. They are not to be construed as reflecting the policy of the Reagan Administration.

WAYNE VALIS
Washington, D.C.
November 21, 1980

ACKNOWLEDGMENTS

I should like first to acknowledge the contribution of Richard Birshirjian, whose brainchild this volume is. Without his support and collaboration it would not have been possible. Invaluable and substantial contributions of time, energy, and counsel were contributed by Professor Gerald Hyman and Hugh F. Young Jr. Major writing contributions were made by John Mueller, and John Lenczowski very generously assisted me in the organization of this book. The editing skills of Professor Noel M. Valis and Susan E. Johnson were most helpful, as were those of Lisa Duperier and William Dowell. I am extremely grateful to William J. Baroody Jr., president of the American Enterprise Institute for Public Policy Research, for his consideration and understanding, and for extending to me the full resources of AEI on this project. Robert Enos and JoAnn Johnson of Arlington House were continually cooperative and reassuring, as also Florence Norton and Peter Landa with their outstanding work in the final production of this book. Nicholas Nichols and Evelyn Caldwell provided me with research materials. Thanks also are due to Karen Bradley and Maura Valis. Finally, however, I owe a great debt to Gabriele Hills and Wendy Kinsman, who rendered yeoman service on the research and organization of this book. Only their forbearance and enthusiastic cooperation at every step made this project possible.

NOTES ON CONTRIBUTORS

WAYNE VALIS is the special assistant to the president of the American Enterprise Institute for Public Policy Research. He served in the White House under Presidents Nixon and Ford, was director of Opposition Research for the President Ford Committee in 1976 and a volunteer for the Reagan-Bush Committee.

ARAM BAKSHIAN JR., a former aide to Presidents Nixon and Ford, is the author of *The Candidates 1980*. A fellow of Harvard University's Institute of Politics, his articles and reviews appear frequently in leading periodicals, including *The Wall Street Journal, The New York Times, National Review,* and *Reader's Digest.*

ROBERT B. CARLESON is currently serving the Reagan Committee for the Transition as liaison for the Department of Health and Human Services. He has served as Commissioner of Welfare in the U.S. Department of Health, Education and Welfare and as director of the California State Department of Social Welfare under Governor Reagan.

DANIEL O. GRAHAM, a retired U.S. Army Lieutenant General, is the author of *Shall America Be Defended?* A former director of the Defense Intelligence Agency, he is presently serving on the American Security Council as cochairman of the Coalition for Peace through Strength.

GERALD HYMAN is a professor of sociology and anthropology at Smith College, a specialist in Asian politics and religion. He is currently a visiting fellow at the American Enterprise Institute.

JACK F. KEMP, a member of the House of Representatives from the State of New York, serves on the economic task force for the Reagan Committee for the Transition. He has served as a special assistant to the Republican National Committee and to the Governor of California, and was formerly a professional football quarterback.

LAWRENCE J. KORB is an adviser on defense issues for the Reagan Committee for the Transition. He is also the director of defense policy studies at the American Enterprise Institute for Public Policy Research. He has been an adjunct scholar at AEI since 1972, and is a former professor of management at the United States Naval War College.

JOHN LENCZOWSKI is legislative assistant to Congressman James Courter (R-N.J.) and lecturer in government and politics at the University of Maryland. A specialist in international affairs, he is author of the forthcoming book, *Soviet Perceptions of U.S. Foreign Policy.*

H. JOACHIM MAITRE, a European writer and journalist, is currently editor in chief of the Axel Springer publishing company in West Germany. He is a former professor of German literature and philosophy at McGill University, Montreal, and a national fellow in residence at Stanford University's Hoover Institution.

JAMES C. MILLER III is the director of the task force for the Federal Trade Commission of the Reagan Committee for the Transition. He is also codirector of the Center for the Study of Government Regulation at the American Enterprise Institute. He has served as assistant director of the Council on Wage and Price Stability and on the President's Council of Economic Advisers.

PEDRO SANJUAN is the deputy coordinator for the Department of State Transition Team for the President-elect. He is director of Hemispheric Studies at the American Enterprise Institute and was formerly a special assistant to the director of the Arms Control and Disarmament Agency.

DALE R. TAHTINEN has published a number of studies and articles on various aspects of Middle East security problems and the American national interest. He was formerly assistant director of foreign and defense studies at the American Enterprise Institute. Dr. Tahtinen was also a foreign and defense issues adviser for the Reagan-Bush Committee and has served with the Defense Intelligence Agency.

I. DAVID WHEAT JR. is the president of Wheat, Luke and Hahn, Inc., a consulting firm specializing in energy policy analysis for refiners, oil and gas producers, and other private sector clients. He served on the White House staff of Presidents Nixon and Ford.

1

INTRODUCTION: THE ONCE AND FUTURE REAGAN

ARAM BAKSHIAN JR.

If Ronald Reagan were in the market for a new slogan, the best choice might be "never knowingly oversold." From the day he first announced his candidacy for Governor of California in 1966, the pundits, pollsters, and political pros have underestimated Reagan in haste and repented at leisure. Whether or not you like his ideas, his positions, or his style, Ronald Reagan has always run better than predicted by the people who are supposed to know. The elitists in the private boxes invariably laugh when he sits down at the piano; the crowd in the gallery invariably ends up giving him a standing ovation. Reagan's landslide victory in 1980 — the first Republican Presidential win with real coattails since Eisenhower's first run in 1952 — is only the latest example of a truly remarkable political career, one that has either defied the smart money or proved that it wasn't all that bright to begin with.

And now that Ronald Reagan has been elected President of the United States, many of the same pessimists have rallied to predict one of two dismal future scenarios: a far-right fiasco in the Reagan White House or a

1

tepid, paralytically "moderate" reprise of the Nixon-Ford years. In the wake of the Reagan landslide, Washington wisenheimers remain serenely confident that they can either discredit or contain a force they first dismissed, then deprecated, and now condescendingly offer to steer.

The joke, I strongly suspect, will be on them. As one who has worked with two Presidents and spent over twenty years observing and participating in politics, I hope that I have enough perception and enough humility to recognize a new political phenomenon when it comes along. Many of my confreres have failed to do so, through pure stubborness, I suspect, or an unwillingness to face facts and realize that while government regulations may be written in Washington, the vital forces of politics in American life remain in the hands of the electorate — a wiser, less naive electorate than the political pros ever thought it to be.

Ronald Reagan has something special. It is a mixture of personal qualities, timing, and the ability to strike a response in average Americans. I am no more capable of pinpointing exactly what it is than is Reagan himself. That's because it is not a contrived act or a conscious pose; it is something in him that is also imbedded in the American spirit, including millions of party Democrats and independents, who broke habits of a lifetime in 1980 to vote not only for Reagan but for Republican senators, representatives, governors, and state legislators.

Anyone who did not know this already could see it clearly on election night 1980 — even in Washington, D.C. What a curious election night it was! It ended almost before it began. By the time the early evening news had been on for ten minutes, the handwriting was on the wall. By eight o'clock, when the doors opened at the Capital Hilton Hotel for what was to have been a nightlong Republican vigil for victory, it was all over. A few minutes later at the Sheraton, where the Democrats were gathered, Jimmy Carter himself bowed to fate and conceded defeat while the polls were still open on the West Coast. The hotel band — out of malice or unconscious irony — struck up "Happy Days Are Here Again."

Sometime between eight and nine that election evening a strange thing happened: "Middle America" descended on the nation's capital. Jubilant citizens by the thousands started pouring into Washington; Chevrolets, Pontiacs, Dodges, Fords, and the occasional battered Volkswagen flooded Connecticut Avenue and the other approaches to GOP headquarters at the Hilton. Most of the tags were suburban — middle-class working people who felt that finally *they* had something to celebrate together. It was the only good-natured Washington traffic jam I have ever witnessed: grandparents, parents, children, grandchildren, bookkeepers, construction workers, housewives, clerks, engineers, small businessmen, and the many other components of America's expanded middle class were cheering, waving Reagan banners, and exchanging greetings from car to car, even as they waited for the traffic to clear.

These were not the big-money people or the power brokers. They were representative of the "silent majority," which had been divided and demoralized in the wake of Watergate. Now they were out in force, even in Washington. And the way they celebrated their night of victory — happily, orderly, and without rancor — said something about them and the man who had led them to victory. It was as if central casting had dispatched a studio full of extras from an old Andy Hardy set. But these people were real, and they had been out there all along, through the bitterness and disappointment of chaos at home, through Vietnam, through Watergate, through inflation, through recession, and, most of all, through the endless liberal propaganda diet of guilt, self-hatred, and defeatism that poisoned the social air of the 1960s and 1970s.

The difference was that now they had a voice, a leader,

a President-elect they believed in and who believed in them.

As the evening wore on, the Democratic casualty list piled ever higher. The tragedy was that there were so few mourners or celebrants. Most depressed Democrats drank early and often and retired prematurely to their beds. Most merry Republicans started whooping it up so early in the evening that they were incapable of appreciating the late night returns that buried such ancient enemies as Frank Church, George McGovern, Birch Bayh, Gaylord Nelson, John Culver, and dozens of other liberal Democratic Congressional wheelhorses.

But the morning after, viewed even through bloodshot eyes, revealed a drastically changed political landscape. Reagan was President-elect, the Senate had a Republican majority for the first time in more than a generation, there was a net gain of thirty-three GOP members in the House of Representatives, four new Republican governors, and substantial inroads in state legislatures.

The political earth's crust had shifted; right was center, center was left, and the left wing of the Democratic Party had been consigned to the outer reaches by blue-collar voters, ethnics, and Southern Democrats, who, regretfully, even perhaps remorsefully, broke away from their New Deal loyalty. Ronald Reagan was the man who led them out.

That was what the first post-election morning showed. But what lies beyond the immediate afterglow of victory? "I will make a prophecy that may now sound peculiar," the immigrant statesman Carl Schurz wrote to a friend in 1864. "In fifty years Lincoln's name will be inscribed close to Washington's on this Republic's roll of honor."

Now it's my turn. Having successfully predicted Ronald Reagan's nomination seven months before the event in my book, *The Candidates — 1980,* and having also predicted a nationwide sweep for Reagan in the general election in the *Los Angeles Herald-Examiner*, I am willing to press my luck one more time. And, like Carl Schurz, I suspect that my latest venture into prophecy "may now sound peculiar" to Reagan friends and foes alike. I predict that Ronald Reagan will prove an effective, popular President, who will work real and needed reforms in government and forge a new moderate-conservative governing coalition. Simultaneously, he will act as a conciliator, a personally trusted, avuncular figure, who will leave office beloved by all but the outermost fringes of the far left and far right.

As I wrote for the *Herald-Examiner* the morning after the Presidential debate: "The Republican Party has *not* yet succeeded in building a permanent alternative coalition of blue- and white-collar workers, 'ethnics,' businessmen and professionals, but it. . . (will) benefit enough from the temporary disaffection of millions of Southern and blue-collar Democrats to evict Jimmy Carter from the White House. . . Only then can the real work of forging a positive new coalition begin." Given the time, I believe Ronald Reagan can and will do it.

To understand *why* he can do it, we have to understand the man himself — his origins, his character, his abilities. Thomas Jefferson once complained that no man brings out of the Presidency the reputation he carried into it. Closer to the truth might be to say that no man takes out of the Presidency qualities he did not bring to the office in the first place. One can learn in office, and one can improve one's *technique* through practice. But the courage, cowardice, wisdom, duplicity, or folly a person demonstrates in office is rooted in the inner self — the differing character and capability innate in each human being. Events may bring these qualities to the surface, but events do not create them. Having studied Ronald Reagan the man, as well as Ronald Reagan the candidate and President-elect, and having viewed him as a historian and biographer as well as a political operative, I see in him the basic qualities of a successful President. Like Franklin Roosevelt, the last great coalition builder, Reagan combines the common touch with remarkable communication skills, a sense of direction, and the ability to lead. Leadership, after all, is not a complicated matter. It works when a leader knows where he wants to go and is able to convince his constituency to follow him — a simple, if not easily achieved, result.

Reagan knows who he is and where he wants to lead us. All the evidence to date indicates that a majority of Americans will follow him on his chosen path, because, as he describes it, it is the one they too wish to follow, the path of national strength, domestic reform, tax relief, and less government interference in everyday life and commerce.

Even Reagan's age — his collective experience of national life over seven decades — strengthens his feel for, and empathy with, a nostalgic American people. Call it a coincidence if you will, but on January 25, 1911, the U.S. Cavalry galloped south to guard the neutrality of the Rio Grande as the bloody Mexican Civil War threatened to spill over into American territory. It was one of the last times that Yankee horse soldiers would ride to the sound of a certain trumpet, a symbolic last post for frontier values and a part of America's innocence. Eleven days later, as the thunder of the cavalry's hoofbeats still echoed in the popular imagination, a child was born in Middle America that would become President of these United States.

He entered the world with a particularly full head of auburn hair, twinkling blue eyes, pink cheeks, an abundance of wrinkles, and a broad grin. His parents named him Ronald Reagan.

Ronald Reagan is the oldest man ever elected to the Presidency, yet his opponents failed to make the age issue work against him. A majority of voters, first in the primaries and then in the general election, concluded

that age without debility is no vice, witness such strik-
ing examples as De Gaulle, Churchill, and Adenauer. Age
in itself brings neither wisdom nor skill, but there are
times when accumulated experience and a calm sense
of history prove invaluable, especially as a stabilizing
force after years of turbulence and drift. Ronald Reagan,
sometimes as a bystander and sometimes a shaper, has
lived through more history than any recent President. It
is hard to realize, when one watches the tall, athletic
Reagan go through one of his polished performances on
the platform or on the tube, that when he was born
William Howard Taft was still President and Teddy
Roosevelt hadn't even begun his campaign as a Bull
Moose, third-party progressive. Reagan was already six
years old when the United States launched itself as a
decisive global power by entering World War I in 1917;
he was only eighteen when the crash of 1929 ushered in
the Great Depression; and he had just turned thirty
when the Japanese bombed Pearl Harbor. Ronald
Reagan has lived through all the major events of the
twentieth century, from the sinking of the *Titanic* and
Russian Revolution to two World Wars, Korea, Vietnam,
and Watergate. Throughout that time he has kept his
eyes open, learned a lot, felt a lot, and experienced a lot
that he can now share with almost every age and class of
America. And that is an important part of leading a
diverse, and often divided, people.

Reagan knows also what it means to be poor and work
his own way up. He was no looker-on during the Depression, he *lived* it. His kickoff speech in November 1979
reflected his deep-felt concern, his usually well-
modulated voice choking up as he described the suffering of his own family in the early 1930s, declaring: "I
cannot and will not stand by while inflation and jobless-
ness destroy the dignity of our people."

He earned a college scholarship and started from
scratch as a sportscaster and then an actor. And at the

age of fifty-five, he overcame the stigma of "show business" to become a successful two-term governor of the largest state in the Union. Like his style and policies or not, no one can ignore the personal achievement involved. A weak man, a stupid man, or a man interested only in his own comfort could not have done it — and probably would not have tried.

Born and educated in Illinois, Reagan was graduated from Eureka College in 1932, with a degree in distinctly pre-Keynesian economics. A former varsity football player, he turned to sportscasting and, in 1937, was discovered by Hollywood. For the next twenty years he was cast in good and not-so-good Hollywood films, usually as a likable, clean-cut type, the sort of character he is in real life. The Hollywood years were not all spent on camera, however. Besides a service stint during World War II, Reagan was active in the Screen Actors Guild, ultimately serving as its president and winning many admirers — and more than a few bitter enemies on the left — for his strong anti-Communist stand. It was his Guild experience, more than anything else, that probably turned Reagan away from his original political alignment as a New Deal Democrat and set him on the road to conservative Republicanism, an experience repeated by millions of independent and Democratic voters in 1980.

In 1964, while all about him others in the GOP were losing their heads, Ronald Reagan became an overnight political superstar, delivering what later came to be known as "The Speech" to a nationwide television audience. It was a standard litany of conservative virtues and liberal sins, but the phrasing and delivery were better than anything else to come out of the disastrous Goldwater campaign, and they won him an instant national following that grew year by year as the message, unlike most warmed-over political rhetoric, rang increasingly true to growing numbers of Americans.

In 1966 Ronald Reagan was elected Governor of California by a landslide, a performance he repeated four years later. In retrospect, he was a good governor of California, that is, a *successful* one. Even in his failures, he was forward- rather than backward-looking. In 1973, for example, he supported a tax-limiting proposal that California voters rejected at the time, but which proved to be the forerunner of Proposition 13.

Ronald Reagan served two terms as governor of one of the biggest, most complex political entities in the world. And he left office popular, no mean achievement in itself and something of a shock to his liberal opponents and the skeptical national media.

After two unsuccessful races for the Presidential nomination in 1968 and 1976, Reagan swept to victory in 1980, winning both the nomination and the Presidency by landslides that took the establishment, the pollsters, and the scoffers by as much surprise as all his earlier political successes.

Will Reagan the President prove an equally positive surprise? Even John Sears, the taciturn campaign manager Reagan fired early in the nominating campaign, has a number of positive things to say about his ex-boss as First Executive. According to Sears, the three cardinal virtues of a successful President are self-knowledge, empathy, and strength in decision-making. Unlike the hollow, vacillating Jimmy Carter, the emotionally tangled and repressed Richard Nixon, or the egomaniacal Lyndon Johnson, Ronald Reagan is a well-adjusted man. He knows who he is and is at peace with himself. This self-knowledge and emotional security make for clear thinking and an ability to work in harmony with widely differing personalities.

As for empathy, Reagan's long and varied life, with its early poverty and struggle and its several successful careers, has brought him into contact with more phases of the American experience, over a lengthier period, than any man to occupy the White House in this century. As an actor, he knows how to empathize intuitively with people beyond the range of his direct personal experience, the very basis of the dramatic art. Given his natural empathy, I suspect that Reagan as President will manage even to bridge the gulf between himself, his party, and black Americans. Because of their disproportionate reliance on the welfare state and the overwhelmingly Democratic affiliation of black political leaders, blacks en masse will doubtless remain in the Democratic column. But once they have had a chance to observe Reagan, in action as President, I believe they will come to accept him as an honest, just man, who seeks to unify rather than divide America.

Finally, there's the matter of decision-making. Ronald Reagan has always been a team player; he has always succeeded in attracting top-notch advisers and administrators and then felt secure enough to delegate real responsibilities to them. Like Eisenhower, he reserves his stamina and his concentration for the really big decisions and big issues — in direct contrast to insecure leaders like Carter, Nixon, and Johnson, who were all obsessed with details and either could not bring themselves to trust, or failed to win the loyalty of, their Cabinet officers. Reagan *likes* people and ideas. He doesn't feel threatened by discussion and debate. As President he will *preside*, which, with a first-class Cabinet working with him, is exactly the kind of calm, measured leadership we need after the many false messiahs of the sixties and seventies.

The ability to reach decisions calmly and to explain them clearly to the electorate should guarantee Reagan strong public support for his efforts to combat inflation, stimulate economic growth, trim government waste, and restore America's prestige abroad through strengthened national defense and a firm, coherent foreign policy.

The economy will be the earliest and most important test of Reagan's leadership. If he can reconcile supply-side Lafferites with free enterprise economic thinkers, and come up with a successful anti-inflationary program, everything else should fall into place, and the collapse of the old Democratic coalition can be transformed into a new, positive Republican consensus. As the syndicated columnist, Joseph Kraft, wrote five days after the election: "Large chunks of the old Democratic coalition have indeed broken off and are now adrift. Reagan can take them in hand — but only on the condition that he masters inflation."

In the chapters that follow you will find detailed analysis, issue by issue, of the kinds of policies, advisers, and organizational structure we can expect under the Reagan Administration. It would be pointless to cover the same ground in summary form here. However, before closing this brief introduction, it might be both rewarding and entertaining to consider the social impact of Ronald Reagan on Washington. One local wag, pointing to the many surface similarities between the Reagan and Eisenhower leadership styles, recently suggested that — *pace* Alvin Toffler — Washington, D.C. is about to undergo "Past Shock." I think it is safe to assume we *will* see a restoration of some of the grace and good manners of earlier days, once Ham, Bert, Billy, Jody, and the rest of the Georgia mafia have been sent back to dogpatch once and for all.

But it isn't just Jimmy Carter's personal clique that is on the run. A quarter century's accumulation of trendy, liberal Senate staffers and senior Washington bureaucrats, even hopeful New Dealers, shopworn New Frontiersmen, and hangovers from the Great Society are even now casting nervous glances over their shoulders and breaking into the coldest of sweats. The mood of the beautiful people has turned ugly.

"Panic Grips Capital!" exclaimed *Washington Post* columnist Henry Allen a few days after Ronald Reagan's landslide. "It's like one of those old horror movies where the atom bomb blast rouses the dinosaurs from the ice they've slumbered in all those eons . . . and all of a sudden you can hear the cry going up in liberal strongholds, from Montessori schools to French bakeries to the Institute for Policy Studies: The Reagan people are coming!"

Allen, who is more of a wit than a political partisan, went on to summon up the mock spectacle of a liberal Apocalypse Now on the Potomac, with area highways clogged by fleeing Democrats and trendies, "jammed to the gridlock with Volvos bearing enlightened folk planning to tough it out on nothing but white wine and Brie . . . leaving no one to brake for small animals or save the whales; no more of the savage culinary competition known as Duelling Cuisinarts; no one left to warm their hands in front of wood stoves, while worrying that a redwood tree might get chopped down."

The cultural counterrevolution is on its way, Allen warned. "Imagine it: Washington returning to those chilling days of yesteryear: life without fern bars, art galleries, French food, gay lib, $250,000 townhouses, pasta machines, Iranian demonstrators, or Bloomingdale's, which is to say civilization as Washington trendsetters have come to know it since 1960."

Personally, I can hardly wait. If a Reagan Administration does nothing else, it will at least bring back leisurely golf and phase out compulsive jogging. Wing tips will replace hush puppies; women will stop cultivating the feminist frump look and begin to dress and groom themselves with a little flair and self-respect again; the First Executive will not address the nation wearing a moth-eaten cardigan; and neither of the Reagan daughters will advise daddy on nuclear fission and the arms race — or, if they do, he won't be stupid enough to quote them in public. Entertainment will range from easy informality to California-style cookouts to polished elegance at state dinners presided over by Nancy Reagan, who is always poised, tasteful, and a treat to the eyes. Cocaine-sniffing and joint-copping will be out, good Cognac and a choice of an after-dinner cigar will be back in.

People won't be ashamed of being successful — even in business — and a President who is attacked by killer bunnies while fishing and collapses while running will be replaced by one who can ride a horse without falling off it. The wine at dinner may not be French, but it will be excellent California Cabernet Sauvignon, and any prescriptions written by doctors on the White House staff will be for real people with real names who suffer from head colds rather than cold turkey.

The Reagan White House's national security adviser won't have a canine taste for publicity; and he won't make a fool of himself with empty gestures or defective machine guns in the Khyber Pass. The First Lady will recognize the fact that the voters elected her husband, not her, to attend Cabinet meetings and conduct the business of the nation. She will be there when he needs her, and will set a tone of subdued glamour and gracious hospitality that will impress foreign visitors and make Americans proud of their First Family.

God will always be welcome at the Reagan White House, but none of its earthly inmates will imply that they have a special hotline to Heaven. We will have a President whose sentences parse, who speaks unbroken English, and who doesn't claim that every celebrity he has ever spent three minutes with is his oldest, dearest friend.

In short, if I am right on even a fraction of these predictions, Americans and our friends abroad will have a lot less to be embarrassed about and a lot more to feel good about when they look at Washington and the occu-pant of the White House over the next few years — the once and future Ronald Reagan.

2

MORAL LEADERSHIP: THE FOUNDATION OF POLICY

JOHN LENCZOWSKI

Ronald Reagan is a moral leader with a philosophy marked by both intellectual and logical consistency. This consistency enables us to identify and even predict the general contours of the vision he has for America.

In essence, President Reagan's philosophy is an assertion of the goodness of traditional American values and institutions and a defense against those ideas and policies that threaten them. These may be divided into three realms: (1) the sociocultural realm; (2) the realm of political economy; and (3) the realm of foreign policy. In each of these areas Ronald Reagan has upheld the merit, the validity, and the efficacy of institutions that have flourished during our nation's history, but which have been eroded in recent years by the ideologies of statism and collectivism. This moral defense signifies above all a pride in these institutions that contrasts with the guilt that has too often characterized a generation of liberal leadership.

Where the recent establishment has proclaimed injustice, seen evil, criticized, "reformed," dismantled, and asserted ever greater power for central government,

Reagan has cautioned, moderated, and fought to conserve those institutions he saw as worth conserving. He has reaffirmed his belief in the essential soundness, wisdom, and competence of the American people. At the same time, he recognizes the intrinsic flaws of human nature and the futility and presumptuousness of attempts to perfect this nature through governmental engineering. Aware of the need for America's positive involvement and influence in international affairs, he has reasserted the wisdom of the traditional American role as defender of the interests and values of freedom around the globe.

President Reagan's faith in the soundness and competence of the people is the basis of his thinking on almost every policy issue. In simple terms, his "can do" attitude stands in stark contrast to the recent sense of helplessness, fatalism, or malaise that has permeated so many ideas about government. Reagan's "can do" attitude, however, refers not to leaving it to government to do it alone, but to letting people solve their problems in their own way. As he has said many times, "We've done it before, and we can do it again."

Rejecting the argument that certain social and international trends are historically inevitable and move in one direction only — that of increased centralized power — Reagan endorses the possibility and necessity of the exercise of free will. He believes that people can change things if they have the will — and the opportunity — to do so. His entire political career of principled perseverance is his testimony to the fact that even one person can make a difference. According to this outlook, success on the personal, national, social, economic, cultural, and spiritual level is achievable. Failure, decline, demoralization, and weakness *can* be avoided.

From this philosophy one major policy change is inevitable in a Reagan Administration: President Reagan will refuse to reconcile himself to failure and will work to help America overcome them. When he says, "Let's make America great again," he means just that.

THE SOCIOCULTURAL REALM
Central to the Reagan philosophy is encouraging the nongovernmental values and institutions of our society. In the campaign this theme was embodied in expressions of support for family, work, neighborhood, and community. To these one might add the various "mediating structures" of society, including churches, charities, volunteer organizations, unions, fraternal organizations, clubs, business associations, and neighborhood groups.

All these institutions, starting with the family, form the fabric of our society. Yet each of them has been the victim of assaults from many directions, most importantly from the government. Government has often seized for itself functions that used to be exclusively the domain of the family and other community institutions. Whereas previously these institutions had sufficient resources to flourish, today government has taxed those resources and assumed the functions those resources once supported.

For example, today the rearing of children is less than ever before in the hands of parents. This is the result of increasing numbers of women seeking work outside the home. An important distinction must be made here. Some women choose to join the workplaces of our nation in an equal and recognized role, which is desirable for society and the millions of women who achieve personal fulfillment in this way. Other women, however, who have chosen family life as their source of fulfillment, are being forced to join the workplace because of the enormous financial squeeze facing American families. It is this situation, imposed on the second group, rather than the aspirations of the first that has put such strain on American families. With both parents forced to work full time to make ends meet, children grow up with less parental guidance. To make matters worse, working wives and their families are subjected to unfair inequities in income, thanks to the "marriage tax."

A solution to these problems, of course, *is* possible, and can be accomplished in ways that both allow career-minded women the freedom and opportunity to realize their goals and enable those women who do not want to be forced to seek employment outside the home to strengthen their family life. This solution, as President Reagan sees it, is to restore to the people a greater portion of the fruits of their own labors. For these are the resources that permit Americans to nurture a strong and healthy family life, as well as constituting the engine of economic growth that affords all Americans, including women, ever greater opportunities for fulfilling careers. So long as government continues to appropriate these resources, neither career women nor the homemakers of our country will have the fullest opportunity to realize their aspirations.

One sees a similar situation in the field of education. Today, control of the education of children continues to slip from the grasp of parents, their neighborhoods, and their communities. Increasingly, the leviathan state centralizes control of education, imposing its values, its fads, its bureaucratic tentacles, and its social engineering schemes. Similarly, the government has done everything to discourage health care of our elderly and handicapped citizens within the context of the home. Medicare and other subsidies are available mostly to those who are institutionalized, while those who remain in the family home suffer unfair financial burdens. Meanwhile, the welfare system encourages and subsidizes the breakup of families, denying children the benefits of parental guidance and perpetuating the vicious cycles of poverty.

Private charitable, volunteer, and neighborhood self-help organizations have been financially squeezed as never before. The highest taxes in our history have curtailed the budgets of the average American so drastically that voluntary contributions become difficult or impossible. Simultaneously, as the state assumes the posture of paternal caretaker of the whole of society, the spirit of private charity and voluntarism is eroded and all but extinguished.

The Reagan Administration will reverse such trends, and will do so by restoring to families, neighborhoods, and community organizations the means by which they can flourish again. President Reagan believes that when these institutions are revived, they can begin once more to play the enriching and beneficial role of which they are capable. For it is these institutions that humanize people rather than treat them as ciphers on program ledgers of government bureaucracies. These institutions inspire the loyalties and responsibilities of people to their fellowmen. Ronald Reagan's vision of the harmonies of the small-town America of his youth is not an anachronism of yesteryear; it is a pattern of human, neighborhood, and community relations that can exist everywhere — even in our largest metropolises, and among people of all races, creeds, and backgrounds — if only those spirits of voluntarism, service, charity, and fraternity can be restored their means of sustenance.

There is one last element of Ronald Reagan's moral philosophy that should be included in this sphere — his philosophy of the ethics of personal versus social responsibility. President Reagan sees a deep strain of moral relativism in our present society, a confusion of our standards of right and wrong. This has burrowed deep into the judicial system and the legal philosophies of many of our lawyers and judges.

Nowadays, when a criminal mugs a senior citizen and steals the twenty dollars in his wallet or loots a hi-fi store during a power blackout, these "new" philosophers proclaim: "It was society's fault!" As the "victim" of society, raised in a bad neighborhood that "society" created, the criminal is allegedly justified in his illegal acts and often allowed to go free — free to commit more crimes against truly innocent victims. As President Reagan sees it, the issue here is not one of right and wrong. It is the total lack of respect for the elementary principle of personal responsibility in a moral context. Under his leadership consciousness of such questions will be restored; for Mr. Reagan recognizes that if our society and its leaders deprive our people, and especially our youth, of socially enforced moral standards, we condemn real and potential criminals to lives of continued personal irresponsibility that will not only victimize society but could well lead to crimes society may ultimately decide to punish severely.

THE POLITICAL ECONOMY
President Reagan's moral leadership extends also to an area sorely bereft of Presidential leadership in recent years: the American political economy.

Central to this philosophy is his belief in the dignity and sovereign rights of the individual. It is this primacy of the individual that represents the bedrock of our civilization's concepts of human rights and true liberal values. And from this belief proceeds Reagan's faith in, and reaffirmation of, our democracy — that it should be the people, in the combined expression of their individual common sense and wisdom, who must constitute the source of our government's legitimacy and direction. What makes this philosophy so appealing is its emphasis on the good judgment of the common people as a sounder and more effective basis of policy than the prescriptions of any self-appointed elite, the only policy yet conceived that guarantees that the people can preserve their freedom.

Indeed, it is the conflict between peoples around the

world and self-appointed elites that underlies the great political and ideological battles of our era. As the forces of democracy and individual rights have retreated in the face of advancing statist and communist elitism, some leaders of democracy have weakened, become demoralized, and ducked the challenge of producing a response grounded in moral conviction. But Ronald Reagan has moral convictions and a response: to stand by democracy and support it unflinchingly.

Essential to this support is upholding the capitalist, free enterprise system. Reagan knows that throughout history there has never been a society rigorously respectful of true liberal values that was not substantially capitalist. As Irving Kristol has noted, capitalism may not be a sufficient condition for a liberal society, but it has proven to be a necessary one. The reason for this, of course, is that the free market is in essence a *democratic* institution. When people have the freedom to choose what they want to demand and supply, they are effectively *voting* in the marketplace in the purest democratic sense. That the people choose — therefore vote for — Big Mac and not veal cordon bleu may not meet elitist standards of excellence, elegance, or sophistication. Nevertheless, it is what the people want, and that is one of the conditions — and consequences — of democracy. Elitists railing out against the mediocrity, philistinism, or prosaic quality of mass culture can still be certain that every possible freedom exists for the pursuit of individual tastes and preferences at their most cultivated.

The democratic nature of the free market economy can be found also in the fact that such a system is decentralized and distributed among millions of economic decision-makers (in fact, all the people) throughout the land. Decisions about how and what to invent, invest, research, develop, risk, produce, supply, save, demand, and consume are made by the people and not by any central authority. And not only do the people have the freedom to make such decisions and be free of unwanted directives imposed from above, but the system works better than any based on centralized decision-making. This is because the people — the marketplace — know, assimilate, and utilize incalculably more information than any elite can process.

That there is social justice in this system is not in doubt, as President Reagan sees it. For it is only through this sytem that the concept of fair trade can operate: equal pay for equal work at prices determined by the people and their values. It is only this system that can produce the rising tide that will lift all boats, both big and small. And it is through such a system of growth, of wealth-creation rather than merely redistribution, that the fruits of human labor can be widely shared to the greater benefit of everyone. Socialist and communist critics will dispute this, of course, saying that such a system does not distribute wealth "fairly" and equally among all the people. What they fail to recognize, however, is that unless people are permitted some freedom to keep a fair share of the fruit of their own labors ("fair" in the sense of the fairness of the trade they make of labor in exchange for compensation), they will not labor as much as they might, with the result that society will be poorer, bereft of the combined production and wealth created by such labor.

Here Ronald Reagan has provided leadership unmatched by any President in decades. Having been one of the first public figures to comprehend the intellectual revolution in economic theory that has taken place in the last five years, he has undertaken the stewardship of this revolution through the policy process in this country. This is the revolution of supply-side economics that has performed a Copernican reversal of the existing demand-side orthodoxies of Keynesianism and Monetarism. Where these theories have focused exclusively on demand (or consumption) as the engine of economic progress, supply-side theory (which is a revival of classical economics) views production and stimulation of human incentives to produce as that engine of growth. Where demand-side theory would cure inflation by taking money out of the consumer's pocket (that is, decreasing demand) and recession by putting money into the consumer's pocket (that is, increasing demand), classical theory recognizes you can't effect both these cures at the same time. Hence our ongoing failure to cure stagflation. Instead, classical theory posits that by stimulating incentives to supply (that is, by offering producers greater rewards for their efforts), economic growth can occur and conquer unemployment and inflation simultaneously.

Intrinsic to the policy of stimulating supply is the policy of putting into use all the various elements of unused capacity. These include unemployed workers, *under*employed workers, capital hidden in nonproductive tax shelters, labor and capital hiding in the inefficient underground and barter economies, and intellectual capital that is diverted from its optimal use by having to cope with the innumerable tax and regulatory burdens imposed by the state. The observation of this tragic waste of human resources has prompted President Reagan to become a moral and intellectual "supply-sider" and to call everyone to the cause of "getting America back to work again." He wants every American to share in the *real* American Dream — the opportunity to rise and develop individual talents to their fullest. When the economy stagnates, that opportunity vanishes. And stagnation is synonymous with the waste of human life.

This is, of course, a comprehensive vision for all Americans, rich and poor, black and white, male and female. It is a vision of self-sufficiency and personal dignity for every American. It is a vision of growth, not only in quantity but in quality: a rising standard of living for everyone.

Ronald Reagan realizes the benefits of growth. That growth is the indispensable condition to creating new jobs at all levels of the economic ladder. The way Americans can enjoy upward mobility, the essence of the American Dream. And upward mobility offers a benefit perhaps even greater than the fuller development of the individual: it protects the people from the entrenchment of a central control, thus acting as one of the great safeguards of our freedom. As growth gives the poor and the unemployed the opportunity for advancement, it simultaneously reduces the need for government programs designed to cope with the effects of poverty and unemployment. Finally, growth makes our country richer. Just as a rich person can afford to buy things more easily than a poor person, a rich economy can afford to buy more legitimately necessary government services than a poor one. To meet our defense needs, for example, we need no longer run the budget deficits that are the source of our inflation.

President Reagan's means of achieving these ends is the reduction of the excessive taxes and regulatory burdens borne by our producers. Despite the efforts of some to label only producers as existing business enterprise, Reagan has recognized that *all* participants — existing business, potential new businesses, and labor — are producers as well. As human beings, the entrepreneurs, managers, and workers of our country all respond to incentives and disincentives. Hence Reagan's stubborn and courageous stand to incorporate his plans for new incentives into his program for reducing not just business taxes but individual income taxes. Individual incomes, after all, form the exclusive basis of the rewards for which producers exert efforts. Confronted with the skepticism and fears of those who protest that tax reduction will cause intolerably large and inflationary deficits, Reagan has stood by his contention that if there must be a choice, a situation of no growth, stagnation, creeping impoverishment, and waste of human life is a graver economic and spiritual threat than a temporarily imbalanced budget. Nevertheless, he has pointed out that in the case of every major tax cut this century the government has gained *increased* revenues from the new growth, increased production, enlarged tax base, and decrease of tax evasion.

President Reagan's plans for tax reduction and eventual indexation of tax rates for inflation comprehend yet another moral dimension, the concept of private property — something he considers to be a natural right. Excessive taxation amounts to an unfair expropriation of people's property. On this ground alone, Reagan feels it must be moderated. But when inflation collides with our progressive tax-rate structure, people are pushed into ever higher tax brackets each time they get a cost-of-living raise. As Reagan sees it, this is a grave injustice perpetrated against a victimized citizenry, a fraud called the "inflation dividend," a dividend to stanch the insatiable budgetary appetite of big government. As people's hard-earned property evaporates from their grasp, and as people get rewarded less and less for the same amount of work, their productivity and America's wealth shrinks. As the underpaid worker in the Soviet Union teaches us: "They pretend to pay us, and we pretend to work."

That President Reagan's philosophy has a "can do" spirit is plain to see. He rejects the vision of a society of no growth in which any attempt to get a bigger slice of the pie comes at the expense of all the other slices. We have seen this phenomenon at work now for several years. Where Americans are discouraged from directing their efforts toward production of more and better mousetraps, enlarging the pie so that there will be more for all, they have been reduced to seeking favoritism and subsidies and fighting red tape in Washington, D.C. Our capital city has become an arena where gladiators from every interest group in America come and cut each other's throats for any crumbs they can snatch from the federal table. Cities are taxed to subsidize the farms. Farms are taxed to subsidize the cities. Society is divided and distracted rather than united and purposeful. And all the while we have been told we are in an "era of limits" and must now learn to live with less — less wealth that must be divided up and administered "fairly" by the holy elite.

Ronald Reagan sees no "era of limits," for he knows that human ingenuity is unlimited. It is a quality that permits us to use limited resources more efficiently and to renew them indefinitely. Ronald Reagan wants to knock down the barriers to American ingenuity so that it might again function freely, at full capacity, and without restraints.

AMERICA'S ROLE IN THE WORLD

The same moral philosophy that animates President Reagan's vision for America at home inspires a policy for America's role in the world. The great question of American foreign policy in recent years has been: Should the United States be a vigorous defender of freedom around the world? A corollary to this is the question of whether, beyond considerations of idealism, it is in our natural interest to play such a role.

Skeptics decided that this role was no longer in America's interest. The lesson they learned from Vietnam was that the defense of people from Communist aggression is a futile, destructive, and immoral exercise, for all it leads to is war, suffering, and opposition to forces for "social change." Moreover, those making pronouncements about our "inordinate fear of communism" saw a grave incongruity in the policy of supporting unpopular and "corrupt" dictators simply because they were anti-Communist. This just wasn't the real defense of freedom.

The result of such views was a foreign policy based largely on guilt. America was seen by them as a force for evil rather than good. Thus it was deemed necessary to behave in a way that would salve our guilty consciences. Where people were being oppressed by a cruel dictator whom the U.S. supported for years as a pillar of anti-communism, we would move to end that oppression. And where "forces of social change" were fighting for liberation or revolution, we would step aside "to let history take its inevitable course," if not actually help the revolutionaries in the hope of "being on the winning side for once."

So came the "human rights" campaign, a policy that would assess the human rights records of all countries that receive American aid. Violators were branded and spanked by denying them aid. Such countries as North Korea, of course, which neither received U.S. aid nor permitted the prying eyes of the Western press or human rights investigators, were perforce ignored by this inquisition. However, the United States undermined the pro-American leader of Nicaragua because he did not meet Wilsonian standards of pure democratic liberalism. Then America joined Cuba in assisting the Communist-dominated junta of Sandinista dictators to replace him. Later, similar policies contributed to the overthrow of the Shah of Iran. In the face of third world accusations of American imperialism and demands for a new international economic order, it was decided that the policy would be to ingratiate and accommodate. And in the face of the Soviet military buildup, the biggest in the history of the world, the policy was to admit that this was a natural and understandable defensive reaction. Since we were the cause of the arms race, then clearly we should practice unilateral restraint and make generous concessions in SALT II. Only then would Soviet fears be calmed and true peace restored to a nuclear world. The Central Intelligence Agency, branded as a den of spies that did dirty things to innocent people, must, of course, be "reformed" and effectively disabled.

The "arrogance" of American power that had caused such harm would once and for all be extinguished.

In the mind of Ronald Reagan these are policies of utter moral confusion, which work at complete cross-purposes to both our values and national interests. Such policies, first of all, are founded upon a gross double standard. Longtime friends, who may be traditional authoritarian rulers but who nevertheless allow many freedoms, are punished for their imperfections, whereas *totalitarian* states with *no* human rights and freedoms are spared criticism and sanctions, are courted and appeased. Quite simply, it was galling to Ronald Reagan to see numerous Latin American friends punished for comparatively minor violations while genocide in Cambodia was totally ignored for three years. He saw this as befuddlement about who our friends and enemies are in the world, in other words, which countries came closer to sharing our values and which countries were competely hostile to our values. What President Reagan clearly recognizes is that unless you have a clear idea of who is friend and who is foe, you can have no coherent foreign policy.

Reagan has also identified another double standard that lies at the heart of this moral confusion, the insistence on measuring American behavior against standards of utopian perfection rather than by comparison with those in the real world. Hence the work of the CIA is condemned, while the crimes of the KGB are ignored. American "imperialism" is vilified, while the Soviet rape of Afghanistan is dismissed.

Ronald Reagan recognizes that the world is not a perfect place and that statesmen can never be angels. He knows that to preserve something of value one often must sacrifice something else of value. This had to be done during World War II. When we had the goal of defeating Hitler, we found it necessary to ally ourselves with, and aid, the equally monstrous Stalin. But we got the job done because we were clear about our priorities and were not hindered by guilt. Reagan also recognizes that there are important moral distinctions to be made between different countries. Some have Berlin walls, others do not; some have Gulag Archipelagoes and boat people, others do not. Under the circumstances, he feels that a true defender of freedom must work to help people without the walls and the Gulags to keep those cruelties away. That this is in our national interest there can be no question. We need friends in the world for access to raw materials, energy supplies, sea-lanes, military bases, ports of call, and other facilities. Any state with a Berlin wall is not likely to be a reliable partner in such ventures.

Ronald Reagan realizes that power is the only instrument through which a country can influence international events in ways congruent with both its morality and interests. He understands that when one country relinquishes power, thus creating moral, political, and military power vacuums, those vacuums will be filled by power and those who have the will to use it. Plainly, those who have demonstrated the will to use power are not always those whose values are congenial to freedom and democracy.

Ronald Reagan believes in the American idea — the idea of democratic capitalism, of growth, wealth creation, opportunity, and freedom. This contrasts with those defeatists who maintain that America "must become more relevant to the forces of change in the world." Characteristic of this position is former Ambassador George Kennan's statement that America "has nothing to teach the world." Ronald Reagan and his supporters could not disagree more. To him such statements amount to nothing less than moral disarmament. In contrast, he would embark in effect on a program of moral rearmament, starting with the reaffirmation and export of the American idea. It is a model for people all over the world, a model that has not been advertised in years, a model of which he is proud.

Armed with the strength of this idea President Reagan will construct a positive and active foreign policy strategy that will once again move to *create* international conditions favorable to the United States and our allies rather than merely cope with events. It will be a policy of crisis prevention rather than defensive crisis management. Utilizing all the neglected tools of foreign policy — sound economic and aid policies, public diplomacy, reliability both as an ally and as an adversary, and renewal of a credible military deterrent — the Reagan Administration will restore American strength in the world. And not military strength alone. More important, since it is founded on true moral leadership, it will be a policy of political strength, the kind of policy that will take full advantage of all the nonmilitary instruments of influence at our command, so that we will never have to use our military ones. In this way we will be able to safeguard our way of life while keeping the peace.

3

RONALD REAGAN: THE MAN, THE PRESIDENT

WAYNE VALIS

Ronald Reagan is now the issue. Will he redeem the broad promise he offered the American people during the 1980 election campaign? Can he launch America on a new course, reversing attitudes of despair and hopelessness grown so pervasive in recent years? President Reagan's formidable task in the early 1980s will be to turn around the vast American government and economy, reducing inflation and unemployment, enhancing productivity, stabilizing the value of the dollar, addressing our energy needs and at the same time remedying rapidly deteriorating foreign and defense policy deficiencies. Above all, President Reagan must restore a sense of optimism about America's future, a sense that America has once more regained its lost vitality.

Unless President Reagan can manage to untangle this web of dilemmas and restore a feeling of forward movement, he will rapidly encounter serious political difficulties. His task is herculean, perhaps insurmountable. And he will be given precious little time.

Indeed, it will be absolutely necessary to hit the decks running, for President Reagan will receive his first report card from the American voter in November 1982. These off-year Congressional elections will be crucial to the success of the Reagan Administration; in fact, could make or break it. Republicans have an excellent opportunity to maintain or even increase their control of the Senate, for in 1982 twenty Democratic seats will be contested as opposed to only twelve Republican. In addition, a gain of about twenty-five seats would give the GOP control of the House of Representatives for the first time since 1954, presenting Reagan with a golden opportunity for carrying out his legislative program. Usually, however, the party in power loses seats in off-year elections. Only in 1934 was the "in" party able to make additional legislative gains. So, should President Reagan fail to convey a sense of movement quickly and show progress in solving issues, in all probability the opportunity to build a lasting new majority will vanish.

Clearly the issue for 1982 will be the Reagan Presidency and the Republican government. The questions will be "Can the Right govern?"; "Can a conservative government effectively organize for and use power?"

To answer these questions we must examine what makes a President successful. We must examine his role as administrator, negotiator, communicator, persuader, and policy analyst. Can Ronald Reagan successfully build and direct a White House staff, deal with the Congress, appoint able individuals to the judiciary, and manage an enormous federal bureaucracy?

The Presidency is both an institution and an individual. His success or failure depends more on his character, intelligence, energy, determination, and personal characteristics than on any combination of personnel management, policies, or programs. It also depends on taking advantage of luck. To evaluate the kind of President that Ronald Reagan will make and how effective his stewardship is likely to be, one must evaluate his personal strengths and weaknesses, and his performance in his years as Governor of California.

What kind of man is Ronald Reagan? Clearly, by all accounts, he is a man of solid, practical intelligence, secure and comfortable with friends, associates, and adversaries. Professor Jeane J. Kirkpatrick is a lifelong, politically active Democrat, who came to know Reagan during 1980, and ended up not only supporting him but becoming a Reagan foreign policy adviser. She describes Reagan as "obviously a nice person," noting that his "fundamental decency" was reflected in his campaign by his "firm disinclination to answer personal attacks, low blows, and demagoguery in kind." She concludes that "because he is a generous, decent person, Reagan can be counted on . . . to unite rather than divide us."

One of Ronald Reagan's strongest gifts is his excellent personal touch and established reputation throughout his career for being charitable. He has almost never exhibited mean and petty qualities, qualities that proved damaging to Presidents Johnson, Nixon, and Carter. They repeatedly demonstrated a thin-skinned sensitivity to criticism, whether personal or political. This engendered in their administrations a "let's get even" mentality, which ultimately undid Nixon and Johnson and seriously damaged Carter's reelection bid. One Reagan associate confided that "Reagan reacts to criticism a lot like Jerry Ford and Dwight Eisenhower. Naturally, he doesn't like it, but he doesn't brood about it. It doesn't aggravate him, and he certainly never lets it fester. Usually he treats it with humor or a joke."

Reagan's humor has always served him in good stead. Whether in press conferences, debates, or in casual settings, he is always ready with a joke or quip. Although this penchant occasionally has caused Reagan press secretaries political heartburn (with an ethnic joke or two), the effect is usually refreshing — not to mention politically beneficial. One extremely telling example of the Reagan wit, and his impeccable timing, occurred during the televised Illinois GOP debate.

In the midst of a strident exchange over whether John Anderson was a true-blue Republican, loyal to his party, or a secret independent (how long ago!), the issue became "would John Anderson support the nominee of the Republican Party." Philip Crane and Anderson thundered at one another. George Bush and Anderson sparked. Finally, it was Reagan's turn to speak. Quietly, he turned to Anderson, fixed him directly in the eye, and earnestly, softly, almost imploringly, said: "But John, you really would find Ted Kennedy preferable to me?" The effect was devastating. The audience, which had been cautioned not to respond, was electrified, their sympathetic laughter and reaction said it all. Post-debate survey polls revealed that viewers named Reagan the overwhelming debate winner. He won a convincing victory in the Illinois primary and removed any doubt about the GOP nomination.

Reagan's charm and self-deprecating wit have always reassured his peers and colleagues — and the voters — that although he is serious about his work, he is never too serious about himself.

Some may sneer at these qualities, calling them contrived or trivial, but they are an important asset in an era of media politics. And certainly today the media play an enormous role in politics. In 1976 each Presidential candidate spent $22.8 million for his campaign, about half of which was expended on television advertising and the media. The media are the filter through which all facts and all realities are perceived by the public.

Without doubt Ronald Reagan will rank with Presidents Kennedy and Franklin Roosevelt as one of the ablest communicators ever to serve in the White House. For good or ill it is imperative (and has been for twenty years) that a President be a good communicator and project a "good image" on television. As a professional actor, of course, he became extremely skilled with television, and at projecting himself to, and establishing empathy with, audiences. In 1964 his speech on behalf of Barry Goldwater raised money and enthusiasm for that sinking campaign and became a legend in political campaign history. It charged up the Goldwater faithful, sustaining them through a disheartening and depressing experience, and propelled actor Ronald Reagan into a political career.

As Governor of California, Reagan repeatedly used television to communicate directly to the people. In 1976, at the Republican convention, Gerald Ford delivered a feisty and rousing acceptance speech, generally regarded as the best of his career. However, Ronald Reagan, called on by a generous President Ford to share the stage and say a few words, unveiled his "shining city on a hill" speech, impressing television viewers and literally bringing tears to some usually very cynical eyes. Throughout 1980 Reagan repeatedly showed his skills as communicator. In the famous New Hampshire GOP debate his justified indignation and forceful resolve to permit all the major Republican contenders to participate stunned and ultimately derailed George Bush's "big mo." In debate Reagan met and bested John Connally, Howard Baker, George Bush, Philip Crane, and John Anderson — articulate men all. That straightforward, congenial, self-deprecating style worked time after time.

An actor's skill? Maybe. But in their finest moments all leaders, including Churchill, MacArthur, and FDR, are combination orator-rhetorician-leader and *performer*.

Contrast Reagan's skills as communicator with his four predecessors. All were able men. But Johnson was ill at ease on television, acutely self-conscious about his Texas accent, large ears and nose, and lack of style. Nixon's "shiftiness," five o'clock shadow, and perspiring upper lip undermined his words; Ford's honest but plain and inarticulate qualities brought undeserved ridicule; and Carter's pedestrian prose, singsong, high-pitched voice, odd phrasing, and peculiar cadences proved distracting and perplexing. Reagan can make an adequate script good; good material he makes excellent. These qualities should enable Reagan to avoid the nasty relationship with the press that plagued Nixon and Johnson, and should permit President Reagan to turn the Presidency once again into what Teddy Roosevelt called a "bully pulpit."

Granted that Reagan will receive high marks as communicator, what of his personal values, intelligence, and managerial skills?

First, President Reagan is clearly intelligent. During his career he has debated Robert Kennedy, William F. Buckley Jr., President Carter, and a host of good Republican rivals. None ever bested him. Reagan's is a solid, practical intelligence, combined with a very strong intuitive sense. It was these qualities, along with his reasonable demeanor, that carried the debate with Carter and finished turning what had been a close race into a thundering landslide.

Reagan's political values are well known and need not be reviewed here. These values stem from certain firm principles he will not violate.

Reagan's character and his vision of America were formed in Illinois during the 1920s and 1930s. The son of Jack and Nell Reagan, Reagan is a product of Midwestern, middle America. This area is closely linked to land and soil, farming and traditional American values. Reagan's father was a shoe salesman, who moved his family from place to place and from job to job. They lived in Chicago and small-town Illinois and were often in difficult financial straits. Reagan's mother was a deeply religious woman, who visited county jails to bring religious education to inmates, singing hymns and sharing the Bible. It was largely through Mrs.

Reagan that young Ronald acquired the strong religious convictions that accompany him to this day.

The result of this Midwestern, middle American upbringing is a very strong character reflecting traditional values. There is very little pretention about Ronald Reagan.

Early on Reagan learned the value of hard work and the importance of a job. After graduating from high school in 1928, he went to a small Christian college, Eureka, located near Peoria. At Eureka he washed dishes in the school cafeteria in order to pay his tuition, which was ninety dollars per semester. In school Reagan was a good student, if more interested in sports and drama than in his major fields of sociology and economics.

But he was interested, even at this early age, in politics. As a son of a Democrat who knew hard times, he also became a Democrat. In his politics, and in college, Reagan was helped by his memory, which everyone agrees is remarkable. He has an almost photographic memory, and had only to scan school materials or scripts to master and absorb them well enough to pass whatever test confronted him.

It is important to note here the lasting influence of the Depression and the experience of World War II on him. Together they gave him a strong sense of fair play, a belief in the value of hard work, reasonableness, and the need for America to be strong. Reagan supported both the "New Deal" and "Fair Deal," strongly opposed the growing Communist movement in Hollywood, ardently supported the creation of the State of Israel, and was committed to a degree of government social and economic activism for the purpose of protecting the poor and downtrodden. Reagan's political odyssey is excellently recounted in *Where's the Rest of Me?* which describes his gradual but growing concern over the size of government and America's role in the world, and ultimately his evolution into a Republican conservative.

The important point is that although Reagan's political affiliation has changed, his ultimate values have not.

Although Reagan the man has rarely been attacked successfully, he is often criticized for his approach to managing. For example, *The Economist* lauded Reagan's choice of advisers, contrasting them vividly with the Carter Georgia operatives, but went on to state: "Mr. Reagan is a good delegator, but not by nature a decisive man. This is probably the most worrying weakness that he will bring with him to Washington." *The National Journal* discussed Reagan's "penchant for staying above the details of government." Reagan's style has been described as a "chairman of the board" type of manager or by one severe critic as "nine-to-five government."

Is Ronald Reagan a good manager, or, as some critics contend, does he lack energy and does he resist learning and dealing with the details of government?

As Governor he delegated, through his chief of staff, Edwin Meese III, "operating authority to subcabinet officials" so that "department heads could serve as personal advisers." I questioned one of those "personal" advisers, Robert Carleson, who was Reagan's welfare director and worked closely with him. Carleson describes himself as a "professional manager," and indeed that was his job before he joined the Reagan Administration. I asked Carleson bluntly whether Reagan was a "nine-to-fiver," and Carleson emphatically responded that "Reagan had a very effective management style," and added, "I was very impressed not only by his organization but also by the way he executed it." Carleson stated that throughout his experience with Reagan, the Governor delegated well, but never abdicated his authority: "He really earned my respect and confidence."

Under Reagan, California received a new organizational arrangement. There were working departments, each headed by a director who reported to an executive cabinet officer. The executive cabinet consisted of eight individuals, who had an extremely close relationship to Governor Reagan, including Ed Meese, the Lieutenant Governor, the director of the department of finance, and cabinet members responsible for human relations, resources (mainly natural resources), agriculture, services, and business and transportation. Thus Reagan had one executive cabinet member for every functional aspect of government.

The overwhelming majority of government business was handled at the departmental, or lower, level. Policy was worked out there and disputes were normally resolved at that level. Important items of business were sent for review to the executive cabinet. If there were disputes at the departmental level, they were almost invariably resolved by the Governor and his executive cabinet. Carleson described most major substantive policy items as routinely going to the Governor and the executive cabinet. He said that the Governor would usually hold two or three cabinet meetings per week, at which all action items were discussed. At these meetings, said Carleson, "the Governor would listen intently and always ask a lot of questions. Usually at these meetings the issue was decided, and, once decided, there was no further appeal. If, however, the Governor felt there was not enough information to make a decision, or if he was unsatisifed with the answers he received to his questions, he would often postpone a decision and request the department head to return with much more detailed information."

However, Reagan tried to prevent controversy or problems from developing by requesting that individual department directors frequently and regularly report to an assigned executive cabinet member for continuing policy guidance. The department directors would routinely call and ask whether proposed solutions were within policy guidelines of the Governor. The executive cabinet member, for his part, would be responsible to see that the latest thinking of the Governor and his administration would be conveyed to the department head and his employees.

Carleson noted that for Reagan this was a very effective management style, one that conserved his energies and permitted him to focus on the most important issues coming before the government. Some of the important elements of that operation were: (1) Only important issues were sent to the executive cabinet and the Governor; (2) if a disagreement occurred at a departmental level, the issues were invariably sent to the executive cabinet; (3) if there were inadequate facts, then the directors of the departments would be called by the Governor for questioning.

Carleson recalled a specific and at the time quite controversial incident. Because of flooding, there was a need for immediate revenues to assist victims. Carleson was instructed to develop a plan to raise such flood-relief funds through a gasoline tax increase. Various formulas were considered, but ultimately the department decided to propose a half cent per gallon increase. "I went to the executive cabinet meeting with my charts and materials. The Governor asked very detailed questions, which proved that he fully comprehended the materials I presented. Finally, after much discussion, he asked about a tax levy for a fixed and limited period of time." The Governor announced that he did not want to raise more tax money than was absolutely necessary to meet the emergency. And he was not in favor of instituting any revenue-raising device that would create a surplus for the general treasury. Therefore, the Governor decided on a tax levy for a fixed period, from six to nine months. The final proposal sent to the legislature gave the Governor the authority to end the tax early so that no surplus would develop. This idea, said Carleson, "was largely Reagan's own brainchild and is an example of his practical cast of mind."

Reagan's former campaign manager, John Sears, takes a somewhat different view about Reagan's decision-making abilities. Sears notes that Reagan is comfortable with the essential responsibility of the Presidency, and is prepared by the "discipline of his former profession to let the critics judge his performance." But Sears contends that Reagan's "decisions rarely originate with him. He is an endorser. It is fair to say that on some occasions he is presented with options and selects one of them; but it is also true that in other instances he simply looks to someone to tell him what to do."

Sears notes that Reagan had not only a very moderate record as Governor of California, but that he had a very moderate and practical manner of decision-making, emphasizing consensus and resolution of conflicts. Sears states that time after time Reagan would simply do what had to be done, acting on a very pragmatic basis. Reagan, he says, is not the type of man to lose sleep over his decision-making. Much like Jerry Ford or Harry Truman, he would weigh the evidence, make a decision, and then simply live with it. Decision-making does not have to be an agonizing process. Sears's "bottom line" on Ronald Reagan: "If his advisers are adequate, there is nothing to fear from President Reagan."

If Ronald Reagan, like Dwight Eisenhower, relies heavily on his staff, then the question is: What kind of talent does Ronald Reagan select? Fortunately, in this area the contrast between Ronald Reagan and Jimmy Carter is enormous.

Ronald Reagan's ability to choose highly qualified talent begins at the top. His two closest aides in the White House will be counselor Edwin Meese III and chief of staff James A. Baker III. Both are successful, extremely mature, and are politically seasoned professionals. Meese was Reagan's chief of staff during his tenure as Governor and has spent the last fifteen years of his life in or around the national political scene. Baker's political experience is equally extensive, centering more in Washington and the federal government. A former cabinet undersecretary in the Ford Administration, he very ably managed Ford's campaign in 1976. After Ford's narrow loss he returned to private practice in Texas, and ran for state office on Governor Clement's ticket in 1978. He then served as George Bush's campaign manager, and after the Detroit GOP convention was recruited by the Reagan campaign. Baker handled all debate negotiations, strategy, and preparation. Both Meese and Baker are intelligent, competent, and well connected with all elements of the Republican Party. Both actively seek advice and counsel from a wide variety of sources, ever broadening their access to new ideas.

In fact, the Reagan Administration will surpass all previous administrations in its use of outside talent. Baker and Meese have already reached out to think-tanks such as Stanford's Hoover Institution, the Georgetown Center for Strategic and International Studies, the American Enterprise Institute, the Heritage Foundation, and others.

As Jeane Kirkpatrick noted: "The knowledge that Presidents need most is the knowledge of their limitations and the knowledge of where and how to find and use experts. Beyond that it is important that a President be willing to consult with knowledgeable and interested parties, to listen, and be able to harmonize diverse perspectives, moderate conflicts, and persuade others to support reasonable solutions."

Contrast the Reagan approach with the Carter approach. In Kirkpatrick's words: "Carter has tried to make himself an expert. After the U.S. embassy was stormed in Tehran, he told *The New York Times* that he spent hundreds of hours studying Iranian history, religion, society, and culture. In the process the President demonstrated how little he understands either about becoming an expert on another culture or about how a President should use his time. Trying to become an expert on Iranian culture because one has a problem in Iran is exactly like undertaking a study of physiology, microbiology, pathology, and pharmacology because one falls ill." As one Reagan intimate put it, "Reagan knows what he doesn't know. Then he gets experts to fill in the gaps."

Reagan also organizes well. His former director of mental health programs, James Stubblebine, stated that Reagan built a "clean, vertical, pyramidical, hierarchical authority structure in which you know where you stand, who the boss is, and who you report to." By all accounts the system worked well. And by all accounts it will be the system adopted in the Reagan White House.

In conclusion, all the signs point to a successful Reagan Presidency. His success as Governor came because he combined attractive personal qualities with skilled political leadership. He consulted widely, including with Democrats, showed moderation and good judgment in appointments, and was able to conciliate and blend diverse political elements into a solid constituency, a very decidedly "non-Republican" constituency at that.

Reagan's task — and opportunity — is to convert his voting coalition in the House and Senate into a governing one. By cementing his new coalition around a core of basic policy issues, he can have profound effects on government and the political structure and usher in the beginnings of a new American renaissance.

4

A REAGAN PRESIDENCY: THE CONGRESS AND THE COURTS

WAYNE VALIS

Ronald Reagan was elected President largely because Americans perceived him as competent. Unfortunately, as pollster Richard Scammon puts it, Jimmy Carter was perceived as "the kind of man you couldn't trust to walk your dog around the block and return with the same animal." The political scientist and Democrat, Austin Ranney, emphasizes the same point and advises President Reagan to provide an immediate contrast with Carter. Ranney thinks President Reagan should make his first official act one of "style." He should make it known to one and all that "his name is Ronald Reagan, not Ronnie Reagan." "Imagine," says Ranney, "President Georgie Washington or Tommy Jefferson or Abie Lincoln. James Earl Carter's first official act was to announce that he would be known as Jimmy Carter. He chose for his name a diminutive, and his administration soon became equally diminutive."

If Reagan is to establish his unquestioned competence as President and a reputation as a successful "doer," he must establish a fruitful *modus operandi* with the Congress. If his Administration is to make an endur-

ing contribution, he must master the even subtler art of
structuring the judiciary. The following sections discuss
Reagan's probable relationships to those two coequal
branches of the federal government.

REAGAN AND THE CONGRESS
One key element in determining the success of Ronald
Reagan's Presidency will be his relationship with Congress. And perhaps no other institution has changed so
much and so often in recent times. In a recent interview
former President Gerald Ford reviewed his thirty years of
service in Washington. The biggest change in government that he had seen has been the shift in the relationship between the Presidency and the Congress, he said.
"Today a President really does not have the kind of clout
with the Congress that he had thirty years ago, even in
matters that affect national security. There is not the
kind of teamwork that existed in the fifties, even if the
President and a majority of the Congress belong to the
same party. The main reason for this change is the erosion of the leadership in the Congress."

The bitter reaction to Watergate and Vietnam caused a
dramatic change in attitudes toward the Presidency and
toward their own leadership on the part of many
members of Congress. The attitude shifted, as one
analyst noted, from that of "don't tie the President's
hands" (under Kennedy and Johnson) to "let's tie the
President's hands, and quickly" (under Nixon). During
the 1970s the Congress passed the War Powers Act to
restrict the power of the President to conduct foreign
policy, enacted the Congressional Budget and Impound-
ment Control Act to restrict the President's control of
the budgetary process, made the President's choice of
an Office of Management and Budget director subject to
confirmation by the Senate, established a budgetary
planning system to rival that of the executive branch,
and generally moved away from the posture of facility

and cooperation (that existed under Lyndon Johnson) toward one (under Nixon, Ford, and Carter) of contention and confrontation.

The Congress also increased the size of its staff enormously. Today it numbers a mind-boggling 23,000. In fact, today's Congress costs over a billion dollars to run. In the interests of "reform" the Congress emasculated the traditional leadership structure and created literally dozens upon dozens of subcommittee chairmen, all of whom purport to be leaders. In 1980 there were 149 subcommittee chairmen in the House, and in the Senate every Democratic Senator, except freshman Senator James Exon, was a subcommittee chairman. All chiefs, and almost no Indians. And at the same time that "reform" weakened the power of the leadership, party responsibility also virtually evaporated. Candidates for the House and Senate generally run on their own with as little dependence as possible on the national party for financing and direction. Although it may not make for effective government, at least in the U.S. Congress it has become true that "every man is king."

This increasingly assertive, but less efficient and less responsive, Congress was what confronted Jimmy Carter in January 1977, and it is what confronts President Reagan today. Are there lessons that can be learned from President Carter's largely ineffective relationship with the Congress, and is there any reason for supposing that President Reagan will do better? Let's look at some recent history.

First, President Carter campaigned as an outsider attacking the Washington system. He bragged that he owed nothing to "special interests," which was quite true. Unfortunately, special interests and the various coalitions that help govern Washington also owed nothing to him. Thus there was a discontinuity between the interests of the President and the interests of those groups who knew far more about what makes Washing-

ton "tick" than did the new outsider President. In no
time they were at loggerheads. In addition, President
Carter made the mistake of choosing for the crucial post
of his Congressional relations director an inexperienced
young Georgian who had served as his state legislative
director and who possessed virtually no knowledge of
Congressional relations, the U.S. Congress, or the Washington scene.

President Carter compounded these errors by clinging
to the mistaken notion that dealing with the Congress
was a matter of simple rationality. His engineer's mind
told him that for every public policy problem there was
one, and only one, solution, which could be discovered
by reasoning together in a sincere (one of the
President's favorite words) and fair (perhaps the President's favorite word) manner. However, dealing with the
Congress has very little to do with engineering. Politics
is an art, an inexact science, a mixture of idealism and
cynicism, of rationality and ego, of principle and self-
interest, of negotiation, arm-twisting, and wheeling and
dealing. President Carter apparently understood little of
this, for he spent relatively little time with members of
Congress. Instead he poured over mounds of paperwork,
devoting hour after hour to detail and minutiae.

Regarding Congressional relations, President Ford
noted: "The President cannot spend too much time with
members of Congress. I think the President has to accept the fact that he must spend more time personally
with members of Congress, and he must work with
leaders of both parties to enhance their strength and influence." Ford notes that the President has to consult
and continually ask the advice of the Congressional
leaders. As former Defense Secretary and Congressman
Mel Laird put it, "you have to make them partners. They
have to be with you on the takeoffs as well as on the
landings."

The master of Congressional relations was President

Lyndon Johnson. The ultimate tactile politician, Johnson went to funerals and weddings, wined and dined members, pinched, hugged, touched, squeezed, drank with, told jokes to, cajoled, wheedled, blustered, threatened, flattered, and generally reached out to members in a physical and direct way. He learned their strengths, weaknesses and vices, and played on each.

Only President Carter of the last four Presidents seemed not to understand that Congressional relations were also a "contact sport." It is very important for any President to show that he knows how to punish as well as reward. Certainly Presidents Johnson and Nixon were famous for making it "perfectly clear" that members who transgressed or hit them with cheap shots would be repaid in kind, usually sevenfold. President Ford was a much more forgiving man, but he certainly believed in waging a hard, clean fight against the Congress when necessary, frequently exercising the veto with telling effect. Jimmy Carter, whose semipacifism in international affairs was almost his boast, was unwilling to use the stick as well as the carrot.

One fine example of Carter's inability to command respect from erring members occurred early in his Administration, when one freshman Democratic Congressman allegedly double-crossed the President on a committee vote on the Administration's hospital cost containment measure. His switched vote defeated the President's proposal in the committee and killed the measure, causing embarrassment and political pain for the President, who had made this proposal one of the centerpieces of his total health plan. One shudders to think of how Presidents Johnson or Nixon would have handled the young fellow. However, instead of punishing the offending freshman, within a matter of weeks Carter had invited him to a White House dinner.

Congressional relations are a ritual that must remain a mystery to "outsiders." Dealing with the Congress is a delicate matter. As one old Washington hand put it, when dealing with members always stick with three rules: (1) Don't try to be funny; (2) don't lie; and (3) don't blurt out the truth.

Why will Ronald Reagan be more successful than Jimmy Carter in dealing with the Congress? First, all available evidence suggests that Governor Reagan was able to work effectively with a legislature controlled by Democrats. Through effective use of one-on-one meetings with the leadership and individual members he was able to impress upon them his goals for California. He also repeatedly demonstrated his willingness to cooperate. Democrats in the California legislature tell of tough but fair fights with the then Governor and an increasingly better working relationship as he continued in office.

In a *National Journal* survey Jesse Unruh, Reagan's rival in the 1970 election and the California Democrat Speaker during Reagan's first term, said that Reagan's record was "not as good as his supporters hoped and better than his critics feared." Second-term Democrat Speaker Robert Moretti discussed Reagan's work in hammering out legislative deals, saying "he was around for the important discussions," and recalls, almost pleasurably, swearing and shouting over tax bills. "We used to decide who would shout and leave the room next; it was kind of a rotating duty to keep the decisions up front." Moretti summed up by noting Reagan's "flexibility" and "behind the scenes compromises," saying "everybody was happy."

Bryce Harlow, an almost legendary behind-the-scenes Congressional relations expert, who has served every Republican President since Eisenhower, predicts Reagan will be successful in dealing with the Congress because of his charm, his warmth, and "his genuine concern for people. He is like Eisenhower. He reaches out, and people are moved. And they can't help but respond."

Just as important has been President Reagan's understanding of the role of the Congress and his efforts from
the beginning of his 1980 campaign to build close ties
with the Congress. Early on Reagan worked closely with
Senator Paul Laxalt, Congressman Thomas Evans,
Congressman Jack Kemp, Senator Howard Baker, and
many others to build a strong working relationship. He
frequently consulted with members and former
members and established a director of Congressional
relations for his campaign. After receiving the
Republican nomination, Reagan increased his ties with
Republican members of the Congress. On September 15
he conducted a meeting, followed by a gathering on the
Capitol steps with most Republican candidates for the
House and Senate, all of whom pledged to form a unified
government. He and these Republicans promised to
take immediate action on a half-dozen major issues as
soon as the 97th Congress opened and Reagan was inaugurated President.

Throughout the 1980 campaign the Republican National Committee sponsored television advertising that
attacked the Democrats for their inability to deal with
the nation's basic public policy problems despite controlling the Congress for over twenty-five years. More
than at any time in the last thirty years the Republican
candidates for the House, the Senate, and the Presidency and Vice Presidency pledged to work together as a
team if elected. They will be judged in 1982 on whether
they have kept this promise. Thus they have a vested interest in effective governing; in fact, the most overriding
vested interest — political survival.

Paul Russo, a young veteran of the Nixon and Ford Administrations, served as Reagan's liaison with the Congress during the campaign. Russo has stated that
Reagan is committed to establishing a strong personal
relationship with the leadership of the Congress. He
notes that President Reagan possesses a universal abili-

ty to communicate his views and to make legislators feel
that their points of view are appreciated, that they are
part of the Reagan team.

As a symbol of Reagan's desire to establish a close
and effective working relationship, he opened his first
trip to Washington after being elected with a daylong
round of consultations on Capitol Hill. Reporter Lee
Lescaze described the November 18 events in the *Washington Post:* "Reagan's visit on his first day in Washington as President-elect was designed to draw a contrast
between his forthcoming administration and the outgoing Carter White House, often criticized on Capitol Hill
for failing to consult Congress. President Carter avoided
the ego-stroking and backslapping of politics on Capitol
Hill, but Reagan's message was that he could and would
take the time to share with Congressional leaders —
Democrats as well as Republicans — the spotlight that
inevitably follows the President. 'What we would like to
do is to resume a relationship based on regular and
rather frequent meetings, in a bipartisan manner, with
the leadership of the House and the Senate,' Reagan
said.

"Judging from the early returns, Reagan's visit was a
hit. The Republican audience has been applauding since
November 4, but even House Speaker Thomas P. (Tip)
O'Neill, Jr. (D-Mass.) had some kind words. 'I liked him
very much,' O'Neill said of Reagan, whom he had never
met. 'I got along with Reagan's staff better than I did
with Carter's staff at my first meeting.' " (It should be
noted that after only a short exposure to the Carter
team, O'Neill bestowed upon Carter's chief of staff the
sobriquet "Hannibal Jerkin.")

A top Reagan aide summarized Reagan's interests in
this way: "We want to avoid Jimmy Carter's fatal
mistake. He never met the power brokers in this city. He
never had any real friends here. Governor Reagan not
only wants to know them, but he needs to get this place

working again" (*Washington Post,* November 19, 1980).

President Reagan has already established a strong staff of veteran Congressional relations experts to work with the next Congress. Former Nixon and Ford Congressional advisers Bill Timmons, Tom Korologos, and Powell Moore, former Congressman Marvin Esch, and a team of Congressional experts will organize a staff that will be a marked contrast to the Carter team.

There will be regular leadership meetings and breakfasts on a bipartisan basis, and all federal executive branch departments and agencies will coordinate their Congressional relations work with those of the White House in order to maximize President Reagan's ability to deal with the Congress.

In addition to these reasons for presuming that President Reagan's relations with the next Congress will be better than President Carter's is the enormously important fact that the GOP now controls the Senate. Thus the Reagan Administration, working in cooperation with Senate Majority Leader Howard Baker, will be able to schedule priority legislation to focus public attention on turning the economy around and reducing federal spending and federal bureaucracy.

The fact that the Republicans control the chamber responsible for confirming Presidential appointees means that for the first several months of the Reagan Administration hearings will be held almost every day on various nominations. A stage will thus be provided for his Administration on which to dramatize its message. Each Reagan Administration nominee, in the course of the questions and answers and personal statements, will be almost certain repeatedly to hammer Reagan's main themes, i.e., less government, reduced spending, tax cuts, and strong defense and foreign policy.

Republican Senators and Congressional staff members will cooperate with Presidential nominees to impress on the Congress and, via the news media, the American public that Ronald Reagan has a prescription for a different and better America. In short, Republican control of the Senate assures that President Reagan, unlike previous Republican Presidents Ford and Nixon, will have an additional visible forum for the articulation of his goals.

In a series of interviews Reagan Congressional relations specialists have indicated they believe one of the early problems of the Carter Administration was the bottleneck that resulted from Carter's attempt to force the Congress to take up numerous complex issues all at once. In the early days of the Carter Administration the Congress was requested to consider, with little advance consultation, an enormously complex energy bill, tax legislation, and welfare reform proposals, all of which bogged down. As a result President Carter suffered political damage, and many senators and congressmen felt that they had been put through the political wringer, with nothing to show for their efforts. Expect President Reagan to show far more restraint in picking targets for immediate Congressional action. A tax cut, coupled with a commensurate reduction in the rate of federal spending, and a possible dramatic showcase for deregulation or restriction of bureaucratic intervention into American life will be picked as "demonstration projects" in the early days of the Reagan Presidency.

There are, of course, pitfalls for President Reagan. First, Democrats, led by able and highly partisan O'Neill, are not going to roll over and play dead. Despite O'Neill's pledge not to criticize Reagan for six months and his statement that "We're not going to come out slugging. We'll be more than fair and lean over backwards," it should be expected that many committees in the Democrat-controlled House will conduct oversight investigations into the Reagan Administration's handling of almost every problem. The Democratic "Young

Turks" will attempt to portray Reagan as a captive of big business and special interest groups. In particular, the Government Operations Committee and the Commerce Committee, staffed by zealous consumer advocates and members of the so-called 1974 Watergate babies class, can be expected to form the nucleus of anti-Republican and anti-Reagan activism.

In addition, there are potential dangers within the Republican Party. For example, some Republican senators and many Republican Congressional staff members, heady with success, having suffered for years under Democratic control, may want to settle scores for perceived slights and humiliations to them over the years. In addition, some GOP senators seem eager to attack on all fronts, to rush through a host of legislation before the Democrats organize effective opposition. Some of the legislation they will propose is certain to be extremely controversial, and will almost certainly alienate important elements of the Reagan constituency, including labor union members, ethnics, farmers, the elderly, and others reaping the benefits of the present entitlement system. Such controversy and confrontation could impair the main thrust of President Reagan's efforts on the economic front, the major front of the political battlefield.

REAGAN AND THE FEDERAL JUDICIARY

President Reagan has a unique opportunity to change the fundamental character of the federal judiciary. In fact, in terms of potentially *enduring* change, the judiciary offers a chance for Mr. Reagan to translate his political philosophy into a new creed of judicial conservatism, which, if realized, could assure an *institutional*, long-term conservative anchor against social policy drift.

This liberal drift has been pronounced both in the issues selected for judicial determination and in the actual disposition of those cases. At no time in American history have more issues, traditionally regarded as political or social, been resolved by judicial decree. The judiciary is often playing the determining role in public policy formulation, superior to that of either the President or the Congress. Alexis De Tocqueville's observation in the 1830s that "scarcely any political question arises in the United States that is not resolved, sooner or later, into a judicial question" is truer now than ever before.

In the last quarter of the century, beginning with the 1954 Brown desegregation decision, the Supreme Court has reshaped much of American political, social, and economic life. The judicial branch has generated changes in such areas as race relations, crime and punishment, Congressional apportionment, women's rights, education policy, land use planning and control, and the environment. School busing, abortion, welfare policy, pornography and obscenity, to name a few, are some of the areas in which the courts have reshaped the political landscape.

Richard Nixon declared that "except for the contribution he may be able to make to the cause of world peace, there is probably no more important legacy that a President of the United States can leave . . . than his appointments to the Supreme Court." And at almost no time in history do so many changes appear to be imminent in the composition of the Supreme Court. Five of the nine Justices on the Court are over seventy years of age, the average age at which death or illness has removed members during this century. As of Inauguration Day, 1981, Chief Justice Warren E. Burger will be seventy-three years old. Associate Justices Lewis F. Powell Jr. and William J. Brennan Jr. will be seventy-four, and Thurgood Marshall and Harry A. Blackmun will be seventy-two. Of these five, four have suffered recent periods of poor health. The twin facts of age and health point to a period of tremendous change on the Supreme Court in the early 1980s. Clearly, President Reagan's appointments will determine the character of the Court for years to come.

Although seven of the nine Justices currently serving were appointed by Republican Presidents, the Court has been closely divided in recent years on a broad range of issues, handing down many five-to-four decisions. The change of even one or two Justices could make a dramatic difference. Just as important, Reagan's Court nominees will be handled by a Senate Judiciary Committee chaired by Strom Thurmond of South Carolina, rather than by Senator Edward M. Kennedy of Massachusetts, the outgoing chairman. Barring disaster, President Reagan's nominations should not suffer the fate of the unsuccessful Nixon battles over the appointments of Harold Carswell and Clement Haynesworth during the early 1970s.

Despite the prospect of being able to reshape substantially the Supreme Court, there are key uncertainties. Recent Supreme Court history demonstrates that rarely have Presidents been successful in stamping their own philosophy on the court. Dwight Eisenhower's appointment of former Governor Earl Warren as Chief Justice is one example. In fact, when asked about his greatest mistake in office, Ike replied: "Two of them are sitting on the Supreme Court." Harry Truman perhaps put it best when he stated, "packing the Supreme Court simply can't be done . . . I have tried it and it won't work . . . whenever you put a man on the Supreme Court, he ceases to be your friend. I am sure of that."

One historical oddity is that President Carter, although he has appointed more lower court judges than any other President since George Washington, has not had an opportunity to nominate even one member to the Supreme Court. Thus he has the dubious distinction of being the first full-term President not to appoint at least one member to the Court.

Although President Carter has been unable to name a

Supreme Court Justice, he has appointed nearly half of all sitting federal judges. This unique situation arose because President Carter was responsible for filling 152 new positions established under the Federal Omnibus Judge Act of 1978, as well as filling an even greater number of vacancies created by natural attrition. The total number of Carter appointees is well over three hundred. Perhaps as important as the sheer number of appointees to the federal bench is the political inclination of the individuals appointed. Many of Carter's appointees have been liberal activists, such as former Congressman Abner Mikva, Ruth Bader Ginsburg, or Patricia Wald.

The presence of these and other liberal activists on the federal bench may cause severe difficulties for President Reagan in his efforts to reduce the stifling burden of government regulation. According to the *Washington Star* reporter, Caroline Mayer: "The courts, public-interest advocates unanimously agree, offer the best hope of success [for keeping environmental and other regulations on the books] because it is the only government insitution where liberal Carter appointees remain." One public-interest attorney pointed out the new game plan by saying, "The courts now loom as the most congenial branch of the federal government. We may have to return to litigation to take advantage of this asset."

Thus, as President Carter departs office, in merely four years he has left an important imprint on the federal judiciary that will continue to shape social policy for years to come.

Since the judiciary is the least visible branch of the American government, and the judge selection process the least understood, let us briefly examine that process.

Bluntly, that process is essentially political. Traditionally, criteria for selecting nominees include ideology, philosophy, competence, merit, and political concerns. These latter include rewarding the party faithful, cultivating favor with influential senators, or winning support from important voting blocks.

Once nominations are decided upon, the President sends them to the Senate Judiciary Committee for confirmation hearings. The record of these hearings is extremely spotty, with few nominees receiving intensive scrutiny. Barring unforeseen controversies, nominations are often approved by the committee without debate, by voice vote, and then reported to the full Senate, where they are usually approved under similar procedures. Thus, the entire judicial selection and confirmation process functions under relatively little scrutiny.

Despite often receiving academic, professional, and political criticism, this selection and confirmation process continued with little change until the 1976 Presidential election campaign. During that campaign President Carter made the revolutionary promise that, if elected, he would choose "all federal judges . . . strictly on the basis of merit, without consideration of political aspects or influences." He also promised affirmative action programs to recruit and appoint minority group members to the courts.

There is no question that President Carter fulfilled his promise in that area of affirmation action, for his judicial appointments include about forty women and fifty members of minority groups. These figures represent more minority appointments than were made by all his predecessors combined.

However, President Carter's record on taking judicial appointments out of the political process and switching to a "merit system" is an entirely different matter. In fact, Jimmy Carter has been the second most partisan President in history. A recent study by Professor Henry Abraham of the University of Virginia, a former Carter supporter, reveals that 97.8 percent of all judges appointed by Jimmy Carter have been Democrats.

President Carter also established a series of supposedly nonpartisan "circuit court nominating commissions," which were supposed to suggest potential nominees to the President based solely on the grounds of "professional merit." However, again according to Professor Abraham, "80 percent of all the commission members have been Democrats," "nearly 50 percent actively supported the Carter campaign (two-thirds of them being pre-1976 convention Carter activists); and over one-third of the respondents were Democratic office holders." For example, the members of the Eighth Circuit Nominating Commission were "composed entirely of Democrats; they had been personally approved by Hamilton Jordan, the President's chief political aide; and its chairman had been an adviser to Vice President Walter Mondale as well as a campaign advance man for Senator Hubert H. Humphrey."

The overriding questions concerning the judiciary now are: What kind of appointments will Ronald Reagan make, and what will be his selection process? His record in California supplied important evidence.

As Governor, Ronald Reagan discovered the truth of President Truman's remark about the difficulty of court packing; and he learned his lesson the hard way. One of the Governor's most important appointments was that of Donald Wright to the State Court's Chief Justice position. Reagan expected Wright to be a judicial conservative, especially on law and order issues and the state's death penalty law. However, a six-to-one opinion of the State Supreme Court struck down the death penalty, with the decision authored by Chief Justice Wright. Reagan publicly admitted later that this decision was a severe disappointment.

Based on past Reagan views and on interviews with Reagan staff members responsible for the judiciary, President Reagan is determined to fill positions on the federal bench with persons believing in what Mr. Justice

Frankfurter called "judicial self-restraint." And if his record is an accurate indicator of the future, Reagan on occasion will exhibit a willingness to depart from tradition in favor of excellence in judicial appointments. As Governor, for example, he refused to accept some nominees of certain state senators for judgeships based on patronage. When the senators offered the argument that they were simply following tradition, Reagan terminated the discussion by simply stating, "the tradition has ended."

Ned Hutchinson, Governor Reagan's appointments secretary, stated that Republican Party membership was considered secondary to nonpolitical qualifications. However, he did state that "if two people are equally qualified for a job, then we would favor the Republican if the other was a Democrat. The Governor naturally would like to see his own philosophy of government carried out by his appointees." President Reagan has made it clear that he will not back away from his principles, which the voters overwhelmingly endorsed. He believes he has a "sacred duty" to implement the philosophy he has espoused for almost two decades. One aide to Reagan declared that the three most important factors in appointing judges will be "merit, judicial philosophy, and judicial temperament."

One controversial factor in this area has been the Republican platform, which calls for the appointment of judges who have "the highest regard for protecting the rights of law-abiding citizens" and whose philosophy "is consistent with the belief in the decentralization of the federal government and efforts to return decision-making power to state and local elected officials." However, the most controversial part of the Republican platform pledges "appointments of judges at all levels of the judiciary who respect traditional family values, and the sanctity of innocent human life."

Although the right-to-life plank has drawn howls of

rage from the pro-abortion lobby, it does not even remotely imply that President Reagan would nominate unqualified or incompetent persons to the bench. Obviously, the platform implies that President Reagan would choose well-qualified judges, nominees who share his own basic constitutional and philosophical convictions. Interpretations to the contrary are not accurate. Judicial history in America indicates that the Republican platform, in this respect, is simply making explicit what has been implicitly sanctioned by tradition over the years. It would be political suicide, as well as politically irresponsible, for Presidents to appoint judges without regard for their political and judicial philosophy.

George Washington, for example, insisted that his nominees to the Supreme Court be strong Federalists, as did John Adams. And so it has been throughout our history. Ronald Reagan seems likely to observe this practice, for it appears that the criterion of judicial philosophy would definitely be considered in his selection process.

As a candidate for the governorship of California, Reagan pledged not to fill state judicial positions "on a basis of personal loyalties or political obligation" and stated that he would "make all appointments to state offices on the basis of experience and qualifications." He promised to promote legislation that would remove the selection of judicial appointments from the political process. To honor his commitment, during his first term as Governor Reagan introduced and worked for the adoption of the California Judicial Selection Act, known as the Merit Plan. The proposed legislation provided for creation of independent nominating commissions that would review all candidates for judgeships throughout the state. The commissions would evaluate the candidates and submit a limited number of names to the Governor, who would then select the final nominees.

Although this plan would have established commissions similar to those instituted by President Carter on the federal level, it should be noted that Governor Reagan did not pretend to exclude philosophy as a determining factor in the selection process.

Although his proposal was defeated, a large number of Governor Reagan's appointments to state judgeships reflected a reliance on an informal merit system. The judicial applicants were screened, and names were sent to groups of lawyers, the state bar, and merit selection panels for advice. Recommendations came back in the form of ratings, and the highest-rated applicant was usually appointed — so long as the candidate was professionally, intellectually, and morally qualified.

Other possible Reagan changes on the Supreme Court would be the appointment of a woman Justice, which he pledged to do at some point in his Administration. Based on his record, he will also support measures to promote greater efficiency in the judicial system, including implementation of more efficient record keeping, calendar management, and other technical matters. These changes will probably be in line with some of the recommendations Chief Justice Burger has made in recent years.

Finally, it should be noted that as Governor of California, Ronald Reagan took great pains to see that the administration of justice was carried out in an honest, scrupulously ethical, evenhanded manner. There were no judicial scandals, à la Billygate, the Marston affair, Bert Lance, Civiletti's conduct, or criticism of his administration of justice. It is also clear that President Reagan will resist efforts by social activists to promote their own political ends through the courts. And given the friendly reception he will receive from a GOP-controlled Senate, perhaps the judicial arena will be the forum for the creation of his most lasting legacy.

5

ECONOMICS, INFLATION, PRODUCTIVITY — AND POLITICS

JACK F. KEMP

At the 1980 Republican National Convention in Detroit I ventured to say: "There's a tidal wave coming — a political tidal wave as powerful as the one that hit in 1932, when an era of Republican dominance gave way to the New Deal. Soon we are going to find millions of Americans of every racial, cultural, and economic background surprising themselves by voting Republican."

Ronald Reagan and a new Republican majority in the U.S. Senate were swept into office in 1980 on the crest of such a wave. Like Roosevelt in 1932, Reagan offered the hope of a better future at a time of crisis. He promised progress toward restoring "full employment without inflation." But, as Irving Kristol has pointed out, "The 'critical election' that established the New Deal coalition did not occur in 1932. At that time people voted for a change — but the exact direction of that change, as well as its dimensions, they neither knew nor foresaw. It was in the first eighteen months of his Administration that Franklin D. Roosevelt, by word and deed, made his election 'critical.' And it was in the Congressional elections of 1934 that the new governing coalition was established as an enduring reality."

In 1952 the Republicans swept into office on a political tide, but were washed back out again in the following elections. The Republicans promised economic and political changes in 1980. How enduring those changes will be depends on how decisively they move within the first twenty-four months to make their campaign goals a reality.

The comparison between President Reagan and President Roosevelt, whom Reagan admires, is a good one. Reagan faces the most severe economic crisis since the Great Depression. Some of the problems are even the same: high unemployment, economic stagnation, and jittery, crisis-prone financial markets. Other problems are of the same nature as the ones we faced half a century ago, but in mirror image. Instead of a sharp worldwide deflation, we have an alarming global inflation; instead of an apparent glut of basic commodities, an apparent shortage. And some problems are new. The most disturbing of these is the slowdown, to zero and less, of the growth in American productivity, and therefore in the American standard of living.

There is one more similarity: The same economic crisis that caused political ferment has also shattered the prevailing consensus of the experts on what the government ought to do about it. Yet this very disagreement gives President Reagan, as it gave Roosevelt, a rare freedom to act boldly in changing the direction of the entire federal government for decades to come.

The consensus that governed economic policy until recently was based on the theories of John Maynard Keynes. Keynesian theory, in turn, replaced the classical theory that had dominated policy-making up to the time of the Great Depression.

Classical theory said that the price mechanism contains a powerful force tending toward equilibrium in the economic market, at the fullest and most productive employment of resources. "In the final analysis, goods exchange for goods," wrote John Stuart Mill. He meant that people offer their goods and services only in order to demand other goods and services. Therefore, if relative prices are free to reflect shifts in supply and demand, the goods and services produced will, in the end, provide the purchasing power with which to buy themselves. Involuntary unemployment — that is, goods and services offered but not demanded — could persist only if there was some obstruction to the adjustment of prices. The government's job, therefore, was to minimize these "rigidities." Otherwise, its motto should be "laissez-faire" — let be, the doctrine of noninterference by government.

To Keynes, the mere existence of the Great Depression was proof that classical theory was wrong, or at least irrelevant. The price mechanism could not be trusted to work in a money economy, Keynes said, except perhaps in the very long run. And in the long run, went his now-famous phrase, we are all dead. The use of money meant, according to Keynes, that supply and demand did not necessarily have to tally. If people hoarded part of their income in cash instead of spending it or lending it to entrepreneurs to spend, there could be less demand than supply. The markets could settle into equilibrium before reaching full employment.

Keynes proposed that the government should counteract this presumed deflationary tendency by expanding the money supply, preferably by financing federal deficits. Although Keynes's thesis of a permanently stagnating economy was forgotten soon after the end of the Second World War, some of his American followers seized on his prescription as a way to maintain full employment throughout the business cycle. The "countercyclical" manipulation of demand, by creating budget deficits during economic downturns and surpluses (in practice, smaller deficits) during booms, was the basic idea of economic policy throughout the Carter Administration.

This Keynesian consensus has been shattered in turn by the failure of its policies to work as advertised. Keynes thought that as long as there is unemployment, "stimulative" monetary expansion can raise only employment, not prices. When this did not prove to be the case, Keynesians tried to salvage the theory by arguing that there is at least a stable inverse relation between the rates of inflation and unemployment, known as the Phillips Curve. Hence, economic policy was seen as a constant choice between the lesser of two evils: higher inflation with lower unemployment or lower inflation with higher unemployment.

The problem is that Keynesian policies have produced a condition that was supposed to be impossible in Keynesian theory: stagflation — simultaneously high inflation and high unemployment. This development has led to a new interest among economists in the classical concern with productivity and supply (which Keynes took for granted) and to a fresh look at the causes of rising or falling price levels.

Modern economists are increasingly convinced that the Keynesian obsession with demand and the tendency to view people only as consumers produced policies that actively discourage employment and productivity. For example, Keynesians advocated steeply graduated income tax rates, not to maximize revenue but to stimulate consumption. Income was to be redistributed from higher income families (who were supposed to save too much) to lower income families (who were thought to be more likely to spend). Instead, steep tax rates on additions to income have merely discouraged everyone from taking on additional work, from saving, and from economic risks. Rather than encouraging economic

growth, attempts to stimulate demand have only accelerated inflation, pushed everyone into higher tax
brackets, and slowed down real economic growth.

FULL EMPLOYMENT . . .

Ronald Reagan and the Republican Party campaigned
on a platform containing specific policies to address our
two fundamental economic problems. One pair of
policies addressed the need to restore incentives for the
fullest, most productive employment of our resources:

1. Tax reform: a 30 percent reduction in personal income tax and capital gains tax rates over three years,
followed by annual adjustments of the tax brackets for
inflation (my own recommendation is for a 40 percent to
50 percent reduction by the end of President Reagan's
first term); liberalized business depreciation schedules
and other tax changes to prevent inflation from raising
tax rates.

2. Regulatory reform: a general effort to remove
counterproductive federal regulation of incomes, like
wages, prices, and interest; and a rationalization of
other federal regulations based on balancing their costs
with expected benefits.

Two other policies addressed the need to stabilize
absolute prices:

3. Budgetary reform: a reduction in the expected
growth of federal spending, beginning with 2 percent in
FY 1981 and cutting at least 7 percent from projected
spending in FY 1985, to balance the budget speedily;
and a reduction in all federal borrowing;

4. Monetary reform: an elimination of excess money
and credit created through the Federal Reserve's purchase of federal debt; and a stabilization of the value of
the dollar in world markets.

Opponents insisted, and some still insist, that these
two pairs of goals are contradictory, at least in the

short-to-medium run. Given the national security requirement to increase defense spending, they said, cutting tax rates and balancing the federal budget can be
achieved at the same time "only with mirrors."

It is worth noting that every candidate who opposed
Ronald Reagan by campaigning on this theme was
soundly defeated. The American people, at least,
seemed willing to try a new approach when traditional
policies were not working. President Reagan and his
economic advisers see their platform not as disparate
and competing policies but as an economic package
that cannot succeed unless all of its interdependent
parts are simultaneously implemented.

Because of the dangerous international situation, we
do not have the luxury of waiting until higher defense
spending would be more convenient; therefore, we must
develop the economic resources to pay for it. Unless the
growth of federal spending is reduced, it will be difficult
to reduce federal borrowing significantly and end inflation. And most decisively, without sound money policies
to stop inflation and regulatory and tax reform to encourage economic growth and jobs, it will be difficult to
control the growth of federal spending.

The new Administration is likely to face a severe
economic and financial crisis during its first year in office. As George Schultz advised President-elect Reagan,
"The federal budget is hemorrhaging." Between June
and November 1980 the estimated cost of the services
in the FY 1981 budget jumped by $36 billion, doubling
the projected increase over the previous year. Respond-
ing to runaway federal borrowing, the Federal Reserve
had pumped up credit at double-digit rates in the
months before the election. This made higher interest
rates, a severe credit crunch, and another recessionary
dip increasingly likely.

President Reagan will find it difficult but possible,
with Congress's cooperation, to achieve his goal of cutting 2 percent from the 1981 budget, or about $13 bil-

lion. Two percent does not sound like much in a $650 billion budget, but much current-year spending has been authorized in previous years. And, taking away the defense budget, payments on the national debt, and automatic federal payments to individuals, this $13 billion must be cut from a remainder of about $160 billion, of which half may be spent or obligated by the time President Reagan can submit his economic program.

Difficult and creditable as this achievement will be, the new Administration cannot stop there. To be credible in its effort to control the growth of spending, the Administration must also lower budget authority now for future years. This is what affects expectations of future inflation, and, therefore, long-term interest rates. Above all, controlling the growth of spending depends on success in reducing the rates of inflation and unemployment. A huge share of federal spending is tied to the "misery index" — the indicators of inflation and unemployment. Of the $36 billion cost overrun between June and November 1980, for example, $26 billion — almost three-quarters — could be traced to such automatic factors as indexed federal benefits, unemployment and welfare payments, interest costs, and other spending triggered by a worsening economy. For this reason a delay or downsizing of the "supply-side" tax and regulatory reform programs would be literally counterproductive.

The federal tax code is essentially the same as it was in the mid-1960s, when our economy was booming, fully employed, and enjoying its last period of relatively stable prices — except for one thing. The tax code was designed for an economy without inflation, and prices have more than doubled in the past dozen years. The combination has raised tax rates across the board on almost every sort of productive economic activity. The personal income tax rates are almost exactly the same as in 1965, but inflation has pushed everyone into higher tax brackets. This process has progressively diminished the incentive to work, and has fallen doubly hard on personal saving; people must save out of after-tax earnings, and then the return on their savings is taxed again. Inflation likewise distorts business depreciation schedules and creates phony capital gains, causing drastic increases in the marginal tax rates on investment.

Inflation also collides with federal price regulations to diminish further the nation's productivity. For example, since world oil prices are quoted in dollars, a decline in the dollar leads foreign oil producers to raise their prices. But the federal government has controlled the price of U.S. oil since 1971 and the price of U.S. natural gas since 1954. The widening gap between the world market price and the controlled American price has caused the United States to consume and import energy too rapidly and to produce it too slowly.

Delaying tax and regulatory reform really means permitting our economy to continue contracting. Is anything gained by doing so, even in the short run? Last year the Senate Finance Committee proposed a bill that would have pared down President Reagan's plan to reduce personal income tax rates by 10 percent in each of the next three years. The Finance Committee bill would have lowered income tax rates a single time, by about 5 percent in the lower half of the brackets and by a percentage point in each of the upper tax brackets. While the bill was commendable in other respects, this provision, though designed to save revenue, would not have narrowed the federal deficit appreciably.

Since the federal income tax was instituted in 1913 there have been two significant and permanent reductions in the tax brackets. During the 1920s Treasury Secretary Andrew Mellon's phased plan lowered tax rates from a maximum of 73 percent to 25 percent. President Kennedy's plan to lower tax rates from 20 to

91 percent to the current 14 to 70 percent range took effect in 1964 and 1965. In both cases IRS records show there was a level of taxpayer income below which the cuts in tax rates immediately lost revenue and above which revenue immediately increased. During the Mellon tax cuts this break-even point occurred consistently at marginal tax rates of 16 to 20 percent. During the Kennedy tax cuts the level corresponded approximately to a 26 percent tax bracket for a typical family of four. This is especially significant because the fraction of taxpayers in tax brackets of 25 percent or above grew from 7 percent in 1965 to 53.4 percent in 1977. There is strong evidence that no revenue is saved by forestalling cuts in excessively high tax rates.

On the other hand, the federal deficit will not be significantly narrowed by making the tax-rate reductions smaller in the lower brackets. Here the problem is not the effect on federal revenue but on federal spending.

Over the years payroll and income tax rates on lower incomes have risen to such a degree that government benefits for not working are increasingly competitive with take-home pay. When the national unemployment insurance system was established in the 1930s, the level of benefits in most states was set at 50 percent of gross wages up to a certain maximum. By itself, this safety net for the unemployed was not a large disincentive to working. Because tax rates on wages were low, 50 percent of take-home pay was almost the same as 50 percent of gross pay. But as payroll and income tax rates have risen, take-home pay has fallen compared with unemployment benefits, which are in general tax-free. A family's income while its chief wage earner is unemployed has risen from an average of just over 50 percent of previous disposable income to about 65 percent, according to a recent GAO study. In fact, a quarter of the unemployed have at least 75 percent of the disposable income they had when last working, and 7 percent actually have more. Another way of saying this is that because of a combination of government tax and spending policies, marginal tax rates facing the unemployed now range from an average of 65 percent to more than 100 percent. The GAO study concluded that more people are unemployed, and for longer periods, because of the change.

Unemployment insurance is partly funded by the federal budget, and is tied to pretax wages. But some benefits are fully funded by federal taxes and indexed to the rate of inflation. When inflation outpaces personal income, as it has recently, workers fall still further behind nonworkers, and every year more workers join the ranks of the unemployed. Over the past decade the minimum level of unemployment at any time has risen from under 4 percent to almost 6 percent.

Each percentage point increase in unemployment widens the federal deficit by almost $30 billion a year in lost revenue and higher spending, according to the Congressional Budget Office. It is, therefore, a delusion to think that the federal deficit can be narrowed significantly without simultaneously cutting marginal income tax rates across the board — regardless of any short-term slowing that may occur in the growth of revenue.

Some argue that the way to improve the worsening trade-off between work and nonwork is to tax or reduce government benefits. But the cause of the problem is not that the safety net is too generous in absolute terms; rather, because of rising tax rates and inflation, the reward for working has fallen.

Ronald Reagan expressed his understanding of this problem in his Detroit speech accepting the Presidential nomination of his party: "We must all move ahead, but we are not going to leave anyone behind." We can and we must reduce the growth of federal spending. But it can be done by drawing people out of the safety net into private jobs, not by cutting benefits in a contracting economy. President Reagan can be expected to make a vigorous effort to cut the fat out of government — but not the heart.

. . . WITHOUT INFLATION

President Reagan's first-term economic package, combining incentives for economic growth and a determined attack on unnecessary government spending, will make it much easier for the Federal Reserve to fight inflation. Inflation results when the Federal Reserve creates an excess supply of cash and credit in the market by purchasing government debt. With a balanced budget, a steady, sound money policy will suffer less from federal borrowing, which preempts private saving and drives up interest rates. The tax reform will also increase the pool of private saving.

Yet balancing the budget alone will not guarantee price stability. Aside from the official budget deficit, the federal government spends more than $20 billion in "off-budget" programs. Various federal credit guarantees and other programs account for approximately $100 billion in additional borrowing under federal authority. And even ignoring the need to bring these federal borrowing requirements under control, what policy should the Federal Reserve follow to maintain constantly stable prices?

There are two schools of thought on the question among President Reagan's advisers. Monetarists generally believe it will be sufficient for the Federal Reserve to maintain a steady growth of the money supply, in line with the long-term needs of the economy. They are generally satisfied with the floating international exchange rates that replaced the Bretton Woods system after 1971. There is common sense in the idea that to stop inflation the central bank must purchase less federal debt. But monetarists cannot agree on the proper definition of money, or on the proper growth rate, or on how to treat dollars held outside the United States. In an era of global inflation, is "the national money supply" any more meaningful than "the Los Angeles money supply" in the United States? Recent experience in the United States and the United Kingdom also questions whether a central bank is capable of accurately determining the quantity of money, which is determined as much by the private demand for cash and credit as by the government's willingness to supply it. And history does not show a single enduringly successful experiment with a managed paper currency.

Another school, including "neoclassical" economists, believes that more fundamental reform is necessary, both to end the inflationary episode of recent decades and to prevent the equally disastrous deflation that concerned Keynes during the 1930s. Keynes, we recall, assumed that a change in people's demand for money — in his theory, hoarding — somehow permits demand to leak into or out of the world economy, independent of supply. Monetarists tend to avoid the problem by assuming that the demand for money is stable. But every properly functioning monetary system, from the classical gold standard to a managed paper standard, contains a mechanism to match supply and demand. A rise in the demand for cash tends to cause a fall in prices and a rise in the rate of interest. Under a gold standard, the coinage authority buys or sells gold on demand at a fixed price. Therefore, a fall in prices causes resources to shift from producing other goods to producing gold, satisfying the increased demand for money as long as it persists. Under a pure paper standard (which the U.S. dollar has been for more than a decade) greater demand for money causes market interest rates to rise until they reach the rate at which the central bank purchases commercial or government debt, creating new money.

The government's monetary target should properly be

the value rather than the quantity of money, say these neoclassicists, so that those in the market itself can determine how much money they need to conduct business at stable prices. This process is disrupted when the banking system finances federal debt rather than commercial needs involving real production. The Treasury should therefore be required to finance its borrowing in the market at the prevailing interest rate, not at the central bank. These economists also believe that the international monetary system should be reconstituted to minimize the possibility of sharp swings in the value of money — whether inflationary, as in the 1970s and 1980s, or deflationary, as in the 1930s. A real commodity like gold should be remobilized as an international unit of account to reestablish stability in world prices and to provide a reliable mechanism for settling international payments.

There is no consensus yet on the scope of the monetary reform that is necessary to bring about lasting price stability. But both monetarists and neoclassical economists agree on one thing: the answer to inflation is to limit the excess creation of money.

In his first trip to Congress after being elected, Ronald Reagan promised to go forward with the proposals on which he compaigned, to "create a prosperity widely shared by all." If President Reagan and the Republicans succeed in implementing their plans to restore incentives for productivity and jobs, to restrain the growth of federal spending, and to reform monetary policy, I have no doubt he will succeed in setting the country back on a course of full employment without inflation.

6

ENERGY: SECURITY WITH CONFIDENCE

I. DAVID WHEAT JR.

Jimmy Carter called his energy program the moral equivalent of war. Ronald Reagan called Carter's program the bureaucratic equivalent of surrender.

Jimmy Carter thought his responsibility was central management of the nation's overall energy affairs. Ronald Reagan doubts that any one person or group — inside or outside of government — is smart enough to improve upon most of the decentralized directions the energy industry receives from the energy-consuming public.

Jimmy Carter's energy bureaucracy tried to cover all the energy bases, but missed the first — government's responsibility to protect its citizens' security and economic welfare when threatened by foreign oil disruptions. Ronald Reagan's energy team will delegate production, pricing, and consumption decisions to the American people so that the government can concentrate on preventing emergencies.

Jimmy Carter's energy policy was best understood by subscribers to the *Federal Register* and analysts of agency organization charts. Ronald Reagan's energy policy will be best understood by television viewers and radio listeners, at home and abroad.

Rhetorical excesses aside, these point-counterpoint observations describe fairly well the salient differences in energy policy perception between the outgoing Democrat and incoming Republican. As this is being written, the Reagan energy transition team is scrambling for office space, telephones, and typists a few blocks from the White House in a herculean effort to prepare the incoming Administration for dealing with OPEC, oil and gas price controls, coal leasing, synfuels, and nuclear power plants, to cite just a few issues on the energy agenda for the 1980s.

As this is being read, the outline of President Reagan's energy initiatives will have begun to take shape. A Secretary of Energy and some of his key advisers will have been named, and also White House staffers who will focus on energy and environmental questions. What in November were multitudes of issue papers will have begun to be transformed into "eyes only" memoranda presaging executive orders, rule-makings, legislative proposals, and speech inserts.

This chapter is not a scorecard of Reagan campaign promises, nor a review of the Republican Party platform. It is not a sneak preview of names and faces, nor a road map for following a particular energy initiative. Above all, it is not an energy-policy prescription. I have three principal objectives: (1) to suggest some criteria for evaluating the effectiveness of energy policy under the Reagan Administration; (2) to describe the economic and political climate within which Presidential decisions affecting energy policy will be made in the early 1980s; and (3) to forecast how President Reagan will define and deal with those energy issues that percolate up to the Oval Office.

ENERGY POLICY CRITERIA

Four years from now the voters' assessment of the effectiveness of a Reagan energy program will not hinge on the amount of governmental sponsorship of either production or conservation, which, after all, are not ends in themselves. One of the many lessons learned from the 1980 election, which turned out of office not only the Democratic Administration but large numbers of well-meaning legislative architects of government programs, is that the American public has learned to distinguish between effort and achievement and has become impatient with politicians who try to fuzz that distinction. Therefore, both idealistic and politically pragmatic appraisals of any energy policy must establish some benchmarks — other than signs of government hyperactivity — against which to measure and proclaim progress.

While the following set of questions may not have exhausted the range of considerations inherent in a national energy policy, the list should reflect the energy-related concerns of most Americans. At the least, it provides a common frame of reference for assessing strengths or weaknesses of President Reagan's energy program.

- Have energy price increases been explosive?
- Has economic recovery, public or private transportation, or home heating/cooling been hampered by inadequate energy supplies?
- Has the health of our economy, the comfort of our homes, or the mobility of our people been adversely affected by foreign oil supply disruptions?
- Has our foreign policy been compromised or unduly provoked by actual or potential disruptions to foreign oil supplies?
- Have oil imports risen as a percentage of total domestic oil consumption?
- Have our sources of oil imports continued to be concentrated in unstable regions of the world?
- Have emergency oil inventories remained at inadequate levels of protection?
- Has the Reagan energy policy adversely affected the

quality of our air and water and the aesthetic and recreational value and geographical integrity of our land?
- Have certain groups of citizens borne a disproportionate share of energy-policy burdens or reaped undue gains at the expense of others?
- Have energy-related government expenditures accelerated?

The pessimistic tone of these questions says something about our national experience during the seventies. As a nation we have come to expect the worst, and energy is no exception. The questions also point up some of the fundamental dilemmas of energy policy — the inevitable trade-offs between price stability and supply adequacy, between environmental protection and resource utilization, and between minimizing government interference and maintaining national security.

Unless the answer to most of the above questions in 1984 is "no," President Reagan's free market approach may get poor marks, notwithstanding (and, regrettably, maybe even because of) undeniable progress on deregulation, energy tax cuts, and DOE streamlining. The American people have had seven years of governmental recipes for mixing programs, procedures, and bureaus by successive self-anointed energy chefs. If never before, the voters are now saying that the proof will be in the pudding.

ECONOMIC AND POLITICAL CLIMATE
Energy Markets. Demand is down and supply is up. So far, so good. Unfortunately, a crisis psychology is at work in world oil markets because of the war between Iran and Iraq, which was well into its second month as the Reagan energy transition team went to work. Nevertheless, despite reports of escalating spot-market crude and product prices as winter approached and fighting

continued, the fundamental petroleum supply/demand situation should be favorable to U.S. interests during Ronald Reagan's Presidency if the war does not spread to other Persian Gulf nations and threaten oil flows through the Straits of Hormuz.

World oil consumption was down nearly three million barrels per day in 1980, with nearly half that reduction coming in the United States alone. With demand dampened by the 1979 price explosion and in 1980 by one of the sharpest recessions in decades, petroleum stocks have reached all-time record high levels. Non-OPEC free world inventories could sustain current consumption rates for about three months even if the Hormuz Straits were blocked.

Despite the expected economic turnaround in 1981, United States oil demand will probably decline another 250,000 barrels per day. Added to the 7.5 percent drop in 1980, this would mean a total decline of nearly 9 percent since 1979. Excluding the strategic petroleum reserve, U.S. stocks are expected to remain nearly 30 percent higher than they were during the three-year period preceding the 1979 price and supply panic in the wake of the Iranian revolution.

Declining petroleum demand should translate into crude oil import reductions on the order of 3 to 5 percent in 1981 (on top of a 16 percent drop in 1980), even though overall U.S. energy consumption should increase slightly (as contrasted with a 2 to 3 percent drop in 1980) as the economy begins to pick up steam.

If the Persian Gulf region becomes embroiled in a wider war, of course, oil deprivation could be stacked on top of oil conservation, and these forecasts would have to be adjusted downward. On the other hand, if the economy expands faster than 2 percent in real terms in 1981, oil demand would probably increase over 1980 and oil imports might turn up again. The unfortunate fact of life is that, in the short run, a fully employed America would be more dependent on oil imports than is the economy Ronald Reagan has inherited from Jimmy Carter.

It is perhaps symbolic that OPEC's twentieth birthday party had to be canceled due to the war between two of its key members. There is certainly less unity within the cartel than at any time since before the energy revolution began in 1973. Saudi Arabia and Iraq have broken relations with Libya, which, along with Syria, has sided with Iran. Algeria has widely criticized Iraq for aggression, while four other OPEC members unquestionably have lined up on the other side.

However, assuming that the current war does not boil over into neighboring member countries — in which case, all bets are off — the outcome of the current struggle should see Saudi Arabia emerge in greater control of OPEC's future than seemed likely at any time in the past two years. The Saudi's long-term pricing strategy for gradually increasing crude oil prices may be on the back burner now, but such moderation is a realistic expectation if the current fighting can be brought under control.

In the minds of most Americans, of course, the energy crisis has been synonymous with runaway oil price increases rather than unemployment. The irony of this public perception of the energy problem is that the bulk of the oil price rise in the last ten years has been confined to two brief periods six years apart. Notwithstanding the infrequency of these jolts and the fact that oil prices were virtually flat in five of the seven years since the 1973 oil embargo, the sustaining public belief has been that in an inflation-racked economy, energy price hikes have led the way year after year.

If the government has a legitimate responsibility to pursue policies designed to maintain reasonable price stability in general — and there is little debate about that — then any energy policy will be judged *in part* by its effect on both the level and change in energy prices. It is reasonable to assume that, since there are no realistic expectations that energy prices would reverse their upward trend within the next four years, a Reagan energy (and economic) policy would receive high marks if the annual rate of increase could be slowed significantly — and if an additional jolt could be avoided.

Even if another market upheaval is avoided during the Reagan Presidency, however, U.S. industry — and, ultimately, consumers — will see oil costs continue to climb steadily in 1981 on account of the decontrol schedule that was set in motion by President Carter in June 1979. By President Reagan's Inauguration Day over 70 percent of U.S. crude oil production will have been freed from price controls, with the remainder scheduled for decontrol between then and September 1981. The new President, of course, has the authority to accelerate that pace.

A little-noticed indicator of energy market happenings is the decline in OPEC's share of the non-Communist world crude oil production in recent years. OPEC's proportion peaked in 1976 at 68 percent, and has declined every year since as a result of increased production principally in three regions — Alaska, the North Sea, and Mexico. In fact, preliminary data suggest that OPEC's 1980 share may be less than 60 percent for the first time since 1970. Of course, not all crude oils are equally attractive as feedstocks. For example, Alaskan North Slope oil is heavier and has a higher sulfur content than crude oil historically refined in the U.S., and, therefore, is not a good substitute for most imports. Nevertheless, the production trend — qualified as it must be — is in the right direction.

Energy Politics. The central feature of domestic politics that makes significant change in energy policy realistic is the new majority status of the Republican Party in the U.S. Senate. Couple that with an apparent conservative working majority in the House of Representatives, and President Reagan has a governing coalition that, as a candidate, he never dreamed would be available.

For months to come serious students of politics will

argue whether Reagan's lopsided electoral college victory was a landslide mandate for fundamental redirection of our nation's policies or merely an anti-Carter phenomenon, since the new President gained only 51 percent of the popular vote. That debate could not be more irrelevant at this point, however, because official Washington, in both parties, *believes* there is a mandate. Warranted or not on a statistical basis, that belief has rapidly become a self-fulfilling prophecy, which, in turn, portends vigorous policy initiatives on key issues across the board, including energy.

The new President's philosophical aversion to oil and natural gas price controls is well documented, and it is virtually beyond question that he will resist an extension of current statutory authority for oil controls when the Emergency Petroleum Allocation Act expires in September 1981. Furthermore, gas price controls under the National Gas Policy Act are scheduled to be phased out by 1985, and it should be expected that President Reagan will seek legislative amendments to accelerate that schedule. Given the Congressional makeup, the President should encounter relatively few serious legislative obstacles during his first two years in office. The partisan Senate support may be relatively stable throughout the full term, since the 1982 elections will again see about twice as many Democrats as Republicans up for reelection. In the House, however, the base of Presidential support may erode somewhat after 1982, given the historical tendency for midterm elections to reduce the partisan Congressional support available to an incumbent President.

PRESIDENT REAGAN'S APPROACH

In the words of candidate Reagan's top energy adviser, renowned wildcatter Michael T. Halbouty, the three ingredients of a Reagan energy program will be "produce, produce, produce." Obviously, in a Reagan Administration this means *anything but* a government exploration and production company. The new President's faith in free market rather than governmental solutions to production, pricing, and consumption problems is established beyond doubt.

How, then, will he proceed to make Mr. Halbouty prophetic? The answer lies in President Reagan's own definition of the "energy issue." Unquestionably, it means to him a problem of exacerbated scarcity, made in Washington by excessive regulation and taxation. Perhaps equally important, President Reagan sees the energy problem as a bitter example of a recurring foreign policy predicament that finds not only U.S. citizens but U.S. security and economic welfare held hostage by actions or threats of foreign governments and terrorists.

If these are his views, what can we expect him to *do*? How will he spend his allotment of "energy issue" time? In short, what components of the energy issue will he view as *his* problems? Finally, since many issues seek out a place on the agenda without having been invited, how can we expect President Reagan to respond to policy dilemmas?

The daily grind of any President is of three types: persuasive speaking to large audiences, carrot-and-stick dialogue in small groups, and solitary homework. President Carter, an engineer by training, considered himself a specialist in the details of analyzing problems and designing solutions — homework, in his view, was his strength. Others considered that same trait his weakness as well, particularly with respect to energy issues, where preoccupation with governmental management of the energy economy frequently left not only him but the American people unable to see the energy forest for the trees.

Like those out of work under a previous technocratic President — Herbert Hoover — the average citizen under

President Carter never expected miraculous solutions. But they did expect their President to help them understand what was going on and to provide a realistic assurance that *somebody* was in charge. Both were disappointed.

President Reagan's gift is persuasive speaking, and that ability is enriched by his grasp of the ebbs and flows of political and economic history. Working with the broad brush of the artist rather than an engineer's pencil, Ronald Reagan will find himself doing what comes naturally: (a) assuring the American people that they are not destined to live in a perpetual energy crisis, and (b) convincing world opinion that America is serious about regaining control of its destiny and never again finding itself over an OPEC barrel.

Ronald Reagan has characterized himself as a New Deal Democrat abandoned by his party. His self-identification with Franklin D. Roosevelt's activist approach to the Presidency and the nation's ills has important implications for energy policy in the eighties.

The new President will shift the public dialogue away from government programs and organization charts and will move vigorously and vocally out front to challenge business and consumers to produce more and consume less, while delivering on his promise to remove many of the government obstacles to both. Since many of his initial authoritative actions might appear negative by current standards — undoing this and releasing that — he will be politically compelled to identify new benchmarks and stress opportunities for results and achievements rather than mere efforts. In so doing, he will be moving with the flow of public expectations.

The sweep of President Reagan's energy initiatives should be evident within a hundred days of his taking office, and will probably occur in two stages. Given that his initial overture to the new Congress will probably be a revised FY 1981 federal budget message, accompanied by the first of what may be several tax-cut proposals, we should get preliminary answers to two broad energy questions: (1) What will happen to the Department of Energy? and (2) What energy tax incentives will get high priority?

It is unlikely that President Reagan will seek early legislative authority to abolish DOE literally, however much that would please him. There are numerous legislatively mandated programs that require DOE administration over the next few years, and a more realistic expectation is that the President would initiate a full-scale reexamination of those programs, seek legislative modifications where necessary, and gradually streamline DOE as changes in its functions permit.

Energy incentive tax cuts, on the other hand, are well within President Reagan's grasp. The biggest target, of course, is the so-called windfall profit tax on crude oil, which, in reality, is an excise tax on production. Because of severe budget deficits inherited from President Carter, President Reagan will probably have to consider cutting the windfall profit tax in successive stages. Whether it can ever actually be eliminated depends on reducing the need for its revenues, which Mr. Reagan obviously hopes to do. In 1981, however, he may concentrate on amendments to reduce the burden on royalty owners and to exempt from the tax certain production from high-cost wells, particularly enhanced oil recovery projects.

Other tax incentives would likely include accelerated depreciation to encourage modernization of plant and equipment to assure greater energy efficiency and alternative fuel conversion capabilities. Crude oil refineries would be a particularly good target for tax relief, given the need to retrofit facilities for low gravity and high sulfur crudes in order to use environmentally acceptable technology to produce light products.

The second wave of energy initiatives will probably

come in April, when the President is required by law to submit to Congress his annual national energy plan. It is in that document that we can expect to see the specifics on accelerated natural gas price decontrol, and a reaffirmation of his commitment to let oil price and allocation controls expire in September 1981. The April message should also unveil his plans for (1) stepped-up oil, gas, and coal leasing on federal lands and the Outer Continental Shelf, (2) streamlining the licensing process for nuclear power plants, and (3) accelerating the completion of the Strategic Petroleum Reserve.

On the foreign policy side, it would not be surprising to see energy-related initiatives, both military and diplomatic, early in the new Administration. With President Reagan's commitment to improve America's defense capabilities may come some well-publicized efforts to better the preparation of U.S. military personnel for protecting vital U.S. interests in the Persian Gulf. Simultaneously, diplomatic overtures to Saudi Arabia would underscore the U.S. commitment to deter Soviet initiatives in the Mideast. One might even look for President Reagan to promote "home energy security" in the same way that civil defense was promoted in the 1950s and early 1960s. The new President will undoubtedly seek a multitude of means for getting across his message that Americans can become more energy self-sufficient and that they should be secure in the belief that their government is using its clout in international markets to prevent another upheaval.

What surprises might he expect? Probably the biggest of all will be the less than unanimous oil industry enthusiasm for immediate decontrol of oil prices and supplies. The lower crude costs available to U.S. refiners have spawned dozens of new small refineries in the past six years, and many will no longer be profitable when the entitlements program ends with decontrol. In addition, both new and established independent refiners will be hard pressed to compete for cost-effective feedstocks so long as some of the integrated majors have a lock on relatively lower-cost crude oils from certain exporting nations (e.g., Saudi Arabia). These are but a sampling of the domestic refiner issues that will surface in 1981, but their common feature is the expressed need for government assistance to withstand product imports subsidized by foreign governments. In addition, crude oil producers engaged in enhanced oil recovery projects currently have a plow-back incentive program available under the price controls program, but capital formation aspects of that program will expire in September 1981. The producers will obviously not be pushing for maintenance of controls, but rather a windfall profit tax amendment that would keep capital flowing to the tertiary projects.

It is also likely that Mr. Reagan has underestimated the inertia of the federal bureaucracy. His efforts to accelerate leasing on federal lands and streamline the nuclear plant-siting process will require changes in long-established procedures in multiple agencies and bureaus lodged within various Cabinet departments and scattered in far-flung regional offices. Suffice to say that straightening out that maze of regulatory roadblocks requires familiarity with the potholes first, and that could take years.

It is doubtful, furthermore, that President Reagan's approach to Cabinet government will make the bureaucracy any less of a problem. An executive committee comprised of the Secretaries of State, Defense, and Treasury, plus the Vice President, Attorney General, and White House chief of staff may be very helpful in keeping the President focused on the nation's most critical issues. However, the bureaucratic jealousy and the compounding of accountability problems that will come with, say, the Secretaries of Agriculture, Interior, and Energy reporting to the Treasury Secretary would be severe.

In somewhat of a reversal of the norm, therefore, it

should be expected that President Reagan will make greater strides in energy policy in the legislative arena than inside "his own" administrative branch of government. Tax incentives for production and conservation and accelerated decontrol may be the most tangible government victories.

To reiterate, however, the energy-policy benchmarks of the 1980s will measure impacts and not efforts. There is a good chance of avoiding another supply and price panic during the early years of the Reagan Administration, and the prospects should improve each year. Energy prices will continue to rise at a steady clip, but additional supplies and more efficient energy use by industry and consumers will be the primary result, with economic recovery relatively unconstrained. Although other scenarios will compete with this one, the prospects are good that Ronald Reagan will get high marks on energy from a confident electorate in 1984.

7

REGULATORY REFORM UNDER RONALD REAGAN

JAMES C. MILLER III and
JEFFREY A. EISENACH

Candidate Reagan made government regulation one of the key issues of his campaign, repeatedly criticizing "wasteful" federal regulations that "impair the ability of industries to compete, reduce workers' real incomes, and destroy jobs." He pledged to reduce the inefficiencies of regulation while preserving its ability to "protect the health and safety of workers, and consumers, and the quality of our environment."

In view of the emphasis Mr. Reagan placed on the issue during the campaign, and because excessive regulation is contrary to his small-government philosophy, it seems virtually certain that regulatory reform will have a high priority in the new Administration. The questions to be answered are: How much will regulation be trimmed? Will reform amount to a simple reshuffling of responsibilities, or will there be fundamental changes in the goals of regulation? How will regulatory reform be accomplished? Will changes in personnel suffice, or will President Reagan seek changes in the underlying statutes? What areas are likely to be emphasized in the Administration's regulatory reform proposals, what will be the reform agenda, and where will be the major battlegrounds?

It is not, of course, possible to predict with certainty the answers to any of the above questions. However, based on analysis of Ronald Reagan's record as Governor of California, his statements on regulatory reform during his Presidential campaign, and, perhaps most importantly, the views of his advisers on regulation, the overall dimensions of the new Administration's regulatory reform program can be discerned.

First, it is important to grasp the character of our problems with government regulation.

NATURE OF THE REGULATORY PROBLEM

Government regulation has expanded rapidly in recent years, from a force that had little impact on the average person to one that directly influences all our lives. From the food we eat to the programs we watch on television, to the prices of many of the goods we purchase, government plays an important role.

Few would suggest that government should have no role in assuring reasonable standards of health, safety, and environmental protection or regulating so-called "natural monopolies." But there is a wide consensus today that the goals of regulation have been set too high, and that the policies aimed at achieving those goals are having little beneficial effect while imposing extremely large costs.

Regulations have been promulgated without sufficient appreciation for the burdens they impose on the economy. The result has been diminished productivity, increases in the rate of inflation, difficulty in starting new businesses, and, most damaging of all, a slowdown in innovation. Partially, this is the result of the inherent difficulty of the problems being addressed and our inexperience in dealing with them. But mostly it reflects the failure of both Congress and the agencies to consider adequately all the effects of increased regulation.

For its part, Congress has passed statutes that place unreasonable requirements on regulatory agencies. In response to concern about air and water pollution, for instance, Congress has passed statutes that are beyond the powers of the Environmental Protection Agency to promulgate and enforce, so the agency is now characterized by an overload of missed statutory deadlines, court reversals, and unenforceable regulations. In other areas Congress has limited the ability of agencies to make economically rational decisions, as is the case with the Delaney Amendment to the Food, Drug, and Cosmetics Act. That amendment requires the Food and Drug Administration to ban from foods any additive that is suspected of causing cancer, regardless of the other benefits the additive might produce. Finally, many of the statutes under which agencies operate are overly vague, containing phrases like "reasonably necessary" and "technologically feasible," for which any number of interpretations are possible.

The regulatory agencies have fallen prey to their constituencies. In the case of the so-called economic regulatory agencies (those that regulate prices and entry in specific industries), the regulated industries usually "capture" the agency intended to regulate them. These agencies in turn have legitimized the otherwise illegal collective pricing practices of these industries and made it difficult for new firms to enter the market. The newer "social" regulatory agencies (those designed to provide for safer products and workplaces and for a clean environment) have tended to be dominated by the interest groups that lobbied for their creation. The EPA, for instance, tends to be populated by those who give proportionately more weight to a clean environment than to other societal goals. The agency is thus prone to discount the costs it imposes in pursuit of its "mission."

Measures of the impact of regulation on the economy are imperfect. However, all of the available measures suggest that regulation, as Governor Reagan said during his campaign, is a growth industry, growing faster than the GNP, the population, or the rest of the federal government. Since 1970 the combined budget of the major regulatory agencies has more than quadrupled; the number of pages in the *Federal Register* has nearly tripled. Economist Murray Weidenbaum, who estimated the cost of federal regulation to the economy in 1976 at $66 billion, now puts that cost at well over $100 billion.

Action by Congress to deregulate airlines and reduce regulation of trucking and railroads may have created the false impression that the flow of red tape has stopped, or even been reversed. The fact is that the new regulatory programs already mandated by Congress, including the Toxic Substances Control Act and the Resource Conservation and Recovery Act, have the potential to impose substantial burdens — perhaps greater than all previous regulations. It has been estimated that the Occupational Safety and Health Administration's proposed generic carcinogen policy might alone provide for regulations costing $55 billion annually. So the prospect appears to be for more, not less, growth in regulation.

PREVIOUS ATTEMPTS AT REFORM

The need to reform regulation has been recognized for some time, and academics and other students of the problem have suggested several means of accomplishing the task.

The most desirable alternative, where possible, is deregulation — the complete removal of the regulations and abolishment of the regulatory agency. This alternative is recommended where competition is likely to serve the long-run interests of consumers better than regulation.

The last four years have seen significant progress

along these lines in the form of partial deregulation of airlines, banking, communications, railroads, and trucking. And the stage has been set for deregulation of energy. But the initiatives to date have been incomplete. In all the areas mentioned above except airlines, the government persists in mandating prices and limiting entry. In other areas, such as maritime shipping and electric power generation, progress toward deregulation has not even begun.

By and large, deregulation is not an answer for the social regulatory agencies. In areas of workplace safety and health and protection of the environment, some government presence is necessary and desirable. The key to reforming social regulation is to create laws, implement procedures, and appoint administrators so that agencies will be encouraged to take into account all of the effects of their actions, including those outside their narrowly conceived missions.

Reform of social regulation has so far produced few success stories. The Carter Administration attempted to require agencies to examine the economic consequences of their actions by calling for Regulatory Analyses of proposed major regulations. This initiative, however, was limited to the executive branch agencies; independent agencies, such as the Consumer Product Safety Commission, were exempt. More important, the program failed to require agencies to pay any attention to the conclusions of their analyses before reaching a final decision. Agencies could do the analyses and then simply ignore them, and all too often they did just that. The Regulatory Analysis Review Group (RARG) and the Regulatory Council, both created at the direction of President Carter in 1978, had no power to force the agencies to do better analyses (in the case of RARG) or to coordinate their activities to avoid overlapping or contradictory regulations (the goal of the Regulatory Council). President Carter's appointees were frequently representatives of so-called "public interest" groups; they were often inclined to pursue their narrow goals without consultation or consideration of the economic impact of their actions.

The Democratic Congress has been reluctant to take meaningful steps to discipline the agencies it created only a few years ago. Although some members have proposed ambitious plans to require agencies to perform benefit-cost analyses that must be incorporated into final agency decisions, to allow the Congress to veto unwise agency decisions, to make regulatory agencies subject to periodic "sunset" review, or to institute a regulatory budget limiting the costs agencies can impose each year, the Congress did not pass a single major social regulation reform bill during the last two sessions. The bill pressed by the Carter Administration, which appeared the most likely of various proposals to win eventual approval, would have done little more than extend the Regulatory Analysis requirement to the independent agencies.

Congress has, however, modified two major individual regulatory statutes. In 1977 it amended the Clean Air Act, and in 1980 it passed the Federal Trade Commission Improvements Act. Both episodes turned into legislative battles between major interest groups. The Clean Air Act amendments of 1977 modified the Clean Air Act to require all coal-fired power plants to have pollution control devices, even if the goal of clean air could be achieved for a lower cost by burning low-sulfur coal. The amendments were a victory for Eastern coal producers, whose coal has a high-sulfur content, but they made little sense economically. The Federal Trade Commission Improvements Act curtailed the powers of the Commission following complaints by industry that its investigations were unfounded. Though the accusations had merit in some cases, the bill failed to separate the chaff from the wheat; it reflected the lobbying power of the industries under investigation as much as the strength of the case against them.

In sum, the results of efforts to introduce economic and administrative efficiency into regulation have shown little success to date. How will Ronald Reagan avoid the problems that have confounded his predecessor?

CLUES TO MR. REAGAN'S VIEWS

During the Presidential campaign Mr. Reagan's opponent made broad claims about his unyielding attitude toward government involvement in the economy. President Carter suggested that, as President, Reagan would move swiftly to emasculate, if not abolish, the major regulatory agencies. The evidence does not support this conclusion.

During his term as Governor of California Mr. Reagan turned a critical eye toward all government programs, including regulation. The evidence indicates, however, that his antigovernment instincts were mellowed by compassion and, in particular, concern for the environment. As Governor, he signed bills creating a state Occupational Safety and Health Administration, requiring environmental impact statements for major construction projects, establishing state control over the location of power plants, and creating the California Air Resources Board. On the other hand, Reagan reacted strongly against regulations he considered unreasonable. In December 1973 he fired three of the four members of the Air Resources Board after it decided to require pollution control devices on used as well as new cars, and replaced them with members holding a contrary view.

Both his campaign rhetoric and the known positions of those on his campaign staff indicate that President Reagan will attempt to cut back on unneeded regulations while preserving the authority of regulatory agencies to issue rules that are truly necessary to protect individuals and the environment. In the area of economic regulation President Reagan can be expected to continue and perhaps even accelerate initiatives to deregulate industry.

Regulation was the subject of a major address delivered by Mr. Reagan on October 8, 1980, in Youngstown, Ohio. In it he called for implementation of a stringent program of cost-benefit analysis of proposed regulations, sunset review of existing regulations and regulatory programs, and development of a regulatory budget. He also promised to review the Clean Air Act to allow increased use of coal in power plants and to eliminate those provisions that discriminate against new plants. Although extremely critical of the Occupational Safety and Health Administration, he has said repeatedly that as President he would not move to abolish the agency.

This collection of statements gives some indication about Governor Reagan's instincts regarding regulation, but little indication about what specific actions he would take. A look at the membership of his task force on government regulation (of which one of the authors is a member) may provide more specifics. This task force is chaired by economist Murray L. Weidenbaum, director of the Center for the Study of American Business at Washington University. Dr. Weidenbaum has been one of the pioneers in the study of government regulation. His text, *Business, Government, and the Public*, is used in colleges and universities throughout the country, and his most recent work, *The Future of Business Regulation*, is widely read.

Though by no means an ideologue, Dr. Weidenbaum has been one of the most outspoken and consistent critics of government regulation. He is a strong advocate of benefit-cost analysis; he believes that regulations should not be promulgated unless the benefits of a rule can be shown to exceed the costs. He has also advocated cost-effectiveness tests. Not only must the benefits of a rule be shown to exceed the costs, the rule must be shown to be the most efficient way of achieving the regulatory objective.

Other members of the task force who have been concerned with social regulation include the second-named author of this chapter, also a strong advocate of a strict benefit-cost requirement, William A. Niskanen, former chief economist for Ford Motor Company and a critic of past regulation of the automobile industry, and Robert W. Crandall, a senior fellow at the Brookings Institution, who is credited by some with developing the regulatory budget concept. All, including Weidenbaum, are former members of the Nixon-Ford Administrations.

Thomas Gale Moore, director of the Domestic Studies Program at the Hoover Institution, is among the members of the task force who have been strong advocates of deregulation in the economic plan. Along with M. Bruce Johnson of the University of California at Santa Barbara, Moore has been active in efforts to deregulate the airline, trucking, and rail industries. Paul MacAvoy, of the School of Organization and Management at Yale University, in addition to his involvement in transportation deregulation, has been an advocate of reform in communications and electric utility regulation.

Antonin Scalia, currently a visiting professor at Stanford Law School, and former Nixon and Ford Administration official, is a student of the regulatory process. He had argued that regulatory agencies are extraconstitutional, since they combine the legislative, executive, and judicial functions in their rule-making, enforcement, and adjudicatory activities, respectively. He has argued strongly against the legislative veto, on the grounds that it circumvents the requirement in the Constitution that both Houses of Congress, as well as the President, must act on all legislation. Robert Bork, professor of law at Yale University; Charles Fried, professor of law at Harvard Law School; and James M. Buchanan, director of the Center for Study of Public Choice at

Virginia Polytechnic Institute and State University, make up the remainder of the team. All are students of regulation and are advocates of reforms that would make regulators more responsible to the public.

WHAT PRESIDENT REAGAN WILL DO
Given this background, we might attempt an educated guess about what policies President Reagan will pursue with respect to regulatory reform. First, vis-à-vis President Carter, President Reagan is likely to deemphasize economic deregulation and focus on reforming social regulations. The reasons are several. For one thing, in many areas economic deregulation is well under way and would not require any substantial input from the President. Also, during the campaign there were widespread reports that Reagan had promised the trucking industry that he would "go slow" with respect to deregulation affecting that industry. Our interpretation is that President Reagan will be no less committed to the ultimate goal of deregulation in trucking, airlines, railroading, communications, and so forth, but that he will show more compassion for those adversely impacted by such deregulation, be more open to policies that would compensate those adversely impacted, and lower the rhetoric on both sides of the issue. (Fairly or unfairly, there was a perception on the part of many in the trucking industry and perhaps the airlines that certain officials of the Carter Administration were more interested in punishing industry than in creating more efficient markets.)

On the other hand, we expect President Reagan to increase significantly the pace of reform in the social regulatory areas. One reason for such an impression is that despite the rhetoric, President Carter and the Congress really did little to address this issue during the past four years. President Reagan seems determined to bring about substantial change.

President Reagan's first major action will likely be the

appointment of "objective" officials to the key regulatory posts. In the past, and especially recently, these posts have been held primarily by proponents of the perceived "missions" of the agencies. Thus, there tended to be a bias in favor of more stringent regulation, and a lack of appreciation for the full ramifications of regulatory initiatives. Although it is unlikely that President Reagan will appoint officials with the opposite point of view — that is, overly antiregulation — the bringing aboard of objective regulators will impart substantial "balance" to the agencies' approach.

The second initiative in the social regulatory area is likely to be support for a version of Senator Dole's amendment to the Senate's languishing regulatory reform bill. The Dole amendment would override existing statutory standards by requiring that before agencies promulgated new rules and regulations they would have to demonstrate on the basis of a reasonable record that these new rules and regulations produce benefits greater than costs and that the least costly alternatives had been chosen. This requirement would be subject to judicial review, so persons in the private sector adversely impacted by regulations could seek redress in the courts if, in their view, the benefits versus cost requirement had not been met. (The key to this requirement, of course, is judicial review, something altogether missing from the currently proposed regulatory reform initiatives.)

Third, we would expect to see President Reagan proposing, after several months, omnibus regulatory reform legislation that would contain provisions to modify each of the major social regulatory statutes. The objective would be to clear away those requirements on agencies to pass regulations that are not cost-effective, and to narrow the agencies' discretion, thus limiting regulatory zeal.

Finally, we may well see President Reagan implementing a one-year moratorium on new rules and regulations. Of course, an executive order to this effect would apply only to the executive branch agencies (independent agencies such as the Federal Trade Commission and the Consumer Product Safety Commission would be exempt), and there are legal questions about whether a President can control the decisions of an executive branch regulator. In addition, there are Congressional and court-mandated timetables for the issuance of certain regulations. Finally, there would be cases requiring emergency regulations. But within this context a modified moratorium might well force agency personnel to evaluate the effects of regulations already issued, free other personnel to formulate needed changes in the enabling statutes, and allow the private sector more time to digest the current crop of regulations.

What would be lacking in President Reagan's policies toward regulation is the indiscriminate slashing of agencies and programs expected, or hoped for, in certain quarters. With the possible exception of the Civil Aeronautics Board — which is currently scheduled for "sunset" in 1985 — no regulatory agency is likely to be terminated during President Reagan's first term in office. But reforms will be made, and evidence of these activities will be clearly felt. For Mr. Reagan has proven to be a man of his word and capable of getting things done. Regulatory reform was established by candidate Reagan as a high priority. In view of that, Americans have every right to anticipate and expect that President Reagan will act.

8

TAMING THE WELFARE MONSTER

ROBERT B. CARLESON

I believe that we have demonstrated in California that a responsible approach to reform of the present welfare system is possible and that given tools, discretion, and adequate financial assistance, states and counties are in the best position to provide a welfare system patterned to meet the real needs of those in America who, through no fault of their own, have nowhere else to turn but to government.

What California has done — other states can do.

Welfare needs a purpose — to provide for the needy of course — but more than that, to salvage these our fellow citizens, to make them self-sustaining and, as quickly as possible, independent of welfare. There has been something terribly wrong with a program that grows ever larger even when prosperity for everyone else is increasing.

We should measure welfare's success by how many people leave welfare, not by how many more are added.

> *Governor Ronald Reagan*
> *February 1, 1972, before the*
> *Senate Finance Committee*

Nearly nine years ago, on February 1, 1972, Governor Reagan testified before the U.S. Senate Finance Committee in opposition to a comprehensive plan to federalize welfare and provide a guaranteed income scheme for all families with children. At that time the family welfare program (AFDC) was out of control. Caseloads were skyrocketing, and ballooning costs were threatening to bankrupt most states. A tremendous strain was being put on the federal Treasury. The plan being considered by Congress was supposed to bring this chaos under control. In addition, its feature of granting cash benefits to intact families was advertised as a means of curtailing family breakups. In his statement in February 1972 Governor Reagan argued that the opposite effects would result if this plan of guaranteeing an income to all families were adopted.

Fortunately for the country and for its families, the Finance Committee rejected that ill-conceived concept of a guaranteed income. Instead, largely as a result of alternative legislation proposed by Governor Reagan and sponsored by the Finance Committee, and actions taken by responsible states following Governor Reagan's lead in state welfare reform, we have managed to tame the family welfare monster. After twenty years of unbroken growth the number of persons in the United States receiving AFDC declined in calendar year 1973, fiscal year 1974, and has declined or remained virtually stable since.

State action has resulted in a reduction in error rates, and the success of the national child support program sponsored by Senator Russell Long (D-La.) in 1974 and, based on Governor Reagan's successful California experience, has surpassed even the predictions made by those who supported this program. Much of this success has been in spite of active opposition by those in H.E.W. (now H.H.S.) and elsewhere who still press for a national guaranteed income scheme.

Moreover, states have been using savings from these successes to increase benefits to those who are truly in need. Example: as a result of California's successful welfare reform program carried out in 1971 and 1972, AFDC recipients received an initial benefit increase of 26 percent after thirteen years of no increases. Cost-of-living increases have resulted in AFDC families receiving in excess of 100 percent more today than they did in 1971, before the reforms, and California's AFDC rolls contained approximately 100,000 fewer persons in January 1980 than in early 1971, when the California welfare reform program started. Mississippi, historically the nation's lowest benefit state, doubled its AFDC basic benefit in recent years.

A massive Seattle-Denver Income Maintenance Experiment, funded by H.E.W. and carried out in conjunction with the state governments of Washington and Colorado, SRI International, and Mathematics Policy Research, has disproved the major contentions of those who support the guaranteed family income plans presented in 1977 and 1979 by the Carter Administration. This major experiment found that family members work less when they are guaranteed a minimum income and that families enrolled in guaranteed income programs are *more likely* to break up than families not enrolled in such programs. In addition, a study undertaken by the Population Division in the Bureau of the Census indicated that the claim made by guaranteed family income plan supporters, that the poor migrate from low welfare benefit states to high benefit states in order to receive higher benefits, is simply not true. Poor people move to find jobs, not to get higher benefits.

Why, then, did the Carter Administration propose and support a new and enlarged version of a guaranteed income for all persons? Carter's massive 1977 reform would have installed in one move a federally administered, Congressionally set, cash assistance program, with universal eligibility based on income only —

all of the characteristics of an efficient system for redistributing income.

The first-year cost of the sweeping 1977 Carter-Califano-Corman bill over the expense of the present welfare system was estimated by the Congressional Budget Office (CBO) to be in excess of $21 billion. Other experts' figures ranged higher; Senator Long estimated a cost of at least $60 billion shortly after the first year. Even the low estimate means a doubling of the cost of the present system. Worse, sixty million people would be eligible for direct, federally administered cash benefits in the first year, compared with twenty-one million now.

When its 1977 comprehensive reform failed to get a hearing before the House Ways and Means Committee because of its obvious high cost and coverage, the Carter Administration introduced in June 1979 H.R. 4904, sponsored by Congressman James Corman (D-Calif.). Jimmy Carter and the plan's sponsors attempted to give the impression that this piece of legislation was a relatively low-cost, compromise reform, costing "only" $3 billion to $5 billion in the first year. They especially did not want to see the bill labeled a "guaranteed income" bill, although that is exactly what it was. It contained the same major elements as the welfare reform plan of 1977. By establishing a national minimum benefit level for aid to families with dependent children (AFDC), mandating that all states include an AFDC program for intact families with the breadwinner "unemployed," and defining "unemployed" in terms of income instead of hours worked, all the key ingredients necessary for a national guaranteed income for families were present.

In addition, by federalizing and liberalizing the assets test and the definition and treatment of income the Carter Administration's program would have reduced the states' role to that of clerks instead of partners. The so-called work requirement was even less stringent than in the present unworkable system. If this proposal had been established, the political dynamics of our represenative democracy would be set in motion with pressures for increased benefit levels, eventually adding millions of persons to the welfare rolls.

GUIDING PRINCIPLES FOR WELFARE REFORM
What, then, is the solution? The solution to the problem should be based on these guiding principles:

Those who are not physically able to support themselves should receive adequate benefits at all times.

Those who, because of advanced age or permanent and total disability, are unable to support themselves, should receive adequate benefits, particularly during inflationary times when their fixed incomes, if any, cannot keep pace with higher costs of the necessities of life.

Those who are not physically able to support themselves should be encouraged and assisted to take treatment or training that may lead to partial or complete self-sufficiency.

Many who are disabled can be retrained or rehabilitated so that they can become productive members of society. Others, through treatment, training, or with supportive services, can become self-sufficient and free of need for institutionalization. Successes in this area bring dignity and self-respect to the individual and benefit all of us through avoiding the high costs of institutional care.

Those who have children should support their children — mother or father, married or not.

In our society the freedom to conceive or bear children should carry with it a responsibility to provide support. Today, over half of mothers with children are working to support themselves and their children or to contribute to their family income. A mother on welfare has as great an obligation to support her children as does the father. The success of the Child Support Program for absent parents has strengthened this principle as it relates to the absent parent. We must do more to see that able-bodied single parents support themselves and their children. Many mothers with several children can provide child care for one or two more in order to free other mothers for work. Once working, a mother can move toward total self-support and, we hope, break the welfare cycle for her family.

No honest work is demeaning. There is no dead-end job.

Those who say that certain types of work or jobs are "demeaning" or are "dead ends" are doing a great disservice to millions of Americans, especially young members of minority groups. This kind of talk is elitist. Millions of good Americans are now supporting themselves and their families in jobs some social planners and "activists" have labeled as "dead ends" or "demeaning." Many millions of other Americans have begun with just such jobs, gained work experience, and as a result have progressed to more advanced work. Millions of aliens, legal or illegal, are now filling many of these jobs, and as a result will advance into more responsible and higher paying jobs, while millions of minority Americans are discouraged from taking them because they are labeled demeaning or dead ends.

Those who know have told us that a restaurant dishwasher who works hard and is dependable is in demand for promotion to busman, waiter, captain, and may start his or her own restaurant. If a "dead-end" job is defined as one where "promotion" is not possible, what about police patrolmen, schoolteachers, factory workers, clerks, salespersons, and others who spend entire careers in the same position, but who get the satisfaction of a job well done and the knowledge that they are supporting themselves, their families, and contributing usefully to their community? After all, in a productive society only a relatively few people can become lead-men, foremen, supervisors, or higher. What is important is not that everyone will move to a more responsible position — that is impossible — but that everyone has the opportunity to do so. Many young people may not have the incentive to engage in any entry level job that consists of hard work in less than comfortable circumstances. If we provide income to them without work, it is only natural that many will choose not to work and will miss the opportunity for future success. If a young man or woman is discouraged from taking a job that would provide valuable work experience and promote the good work habits necessary in the competition for advancement because the job is "demeaning" or "dead-ended," the victim is that young person — and society.

For an able-bodied person to take something for nothing is demeaning.

In a free society we all have the right to live our own lives in freedom as long as we don't impinge on the freedom of others. We may or may not have children. We may travel as we choose. We are obligated, however, to support ourselves and our children to the best of our ability as a price for this freedom. In a totalitarian state we would not have the freedom *or* the responsibility to do so. We also have an obligation to provide for common needs and to provide support for those in our society who through adversity or misfortune *cannot* help themselves. No responsible American would have it any other way. Therefore, productive citizens pay taxes to support the disabled. If an able-bodied person does not do everything he or she can to support himself and his family, and instead takes support from those citizens who are working to support themselves and their families, it not only debases and demeans that person, it places an unfair burden on the tax-paying workers. Even worse, when government decides that a person who is working, supporting his or her family with pride, and gaining respect from the family is not providing *enough* and is therefore guaranteed a "sufficient" income from government, that person loses self-respect and the respect of his or her family. As the Seattle-Denver Income Maintenance Experiment indicated, this can be a tragic cause of family breakup.

The economy, and therefore the poor, cannot survive in a system that pays able-bodied people something for doing nothing.

We hear continually about the millions of illegal aliens working in this country. It is true that some are being exploited, but the vast majority are taking jobs that, we are told, "Americans don't want." These often are jobs at or above the minimum wage. At the same time, employers are continually complaining that they cannot find willing, reliable workers even in our central cities, where unemployment rates are high. Our country's rate of productivity is lagging behind several other industrialized nations, in good measure because we have structured a welfare system that pays able-bodied people for doing nothing. In fact, it often pays more than many entry level jobs. Many employers, especially those with small businesses, cannot compete with some of these high welfare benefits. As a result, jobs are lost or not created. A job in the private sector is preferable to a "created" public job. Federal guaranteed income programs as proposed by the Carter Administration would move in the same direction and would, after enacted, cause annual pressures on future Congresses to increase the minimum benefits continually until the nation's economy collapses. Instead of the poor getting more, *everyone* will get less.

Those who are able-bodied should work for their benefits.

As Martin Anderson, President-elect Reagan's principle domestic policy adviser, explains so ably in his book, *Welfare*, we have not yet found the mix of benefits and incentives that will provide for really basic human needs and yet will not discourage gainful employment. The higher the benefit rate, the more people will find it economically preferable to take welfare instead of a job. Despite their long record of generosity to the truly needy, the American people do not expect their welfare system to provide benefits to those who will not help themselves. The message of the recent welfare work requirement in Bordentown, New Jersey, is that able-bodied welfare recipients will find jobs when it is made clear to them that they are expected to earn their benefits.

Local and state governments are uniquely suited to do the job, provided necessary resources are made available to them.

A welfare system that embraces these guiding principles cannot be designed or run from Washington — particularly from the Department of Health and Human Services. Whether someone is able-bodied or not, working or not, absent or not cannot be determined from a central office on Independence Avenue. Providing work, child care, or supportive services can be done only in the state or community where the people live. Benefits or work availability should start when and where need starts, and benefits should end when need ends. Benefit levels should be adequate to meet basic needs at all times, but should not compete with an area's prevailing wages for those who are able-bodied. Rather, therefore, than moving toward more federal control over welfare as proposed in the Carter Administration's bill, we should move toward less federal and more state control.

The present open-ended matching structure of financing the AFDC program, however, tends to minimize the incentive for states to make their programs more effective. The federal government assumes a large portion (50 to 80 percent) of state costs on a completely open-ended basis. The more states spend or waste, the more federal money comes into the states. On the other hand, when states cut down on spending by eliminating waste or moving people from welfare to employment, they lose federal matching funds. The whole system rewards waste and penalizes frugal economical management. Proposals to provide fiscal relief to states by way of increased matching funds would only worsen this situation.

By using a block grant funding approach instead of a matching approach, the incentive can be reversed. The amount of the grant can be established at the level required to replace present federal funding with whatever additional amount for fiscal relief may be found necessary. That grant level, once established for a state and indexed for inflation, population changes, and unusually high unemployment, would remain in place without regard to increases or decreases in the state's caseload. This would give each state the strongest possible incentive to improve the operation and structure of its program. If an ineligible person were kept off the rolls, or an eligible person given a job, the full amount saved would be available to the state to use for increasing the grants to eligible persons or for whatever purpose the state found appropriate.

The Family Welfare Improvement Act, S.1382, introduced in the Senate by Senators Russell Long, Bob Dole, Robert Packwood, Richard Schweiker, S.I. Hayakawa, and others, and its companion bill, H.R.4460, introduced in the House by Congressmen Barber Conable (R-N.Y.), John Rousselot (R-Calif.), and others, offer steps toward greater state innovation and control. This legislation would replace the present open-ended AFDC matching system with a block grant, provide additional funds for fiscal relief, and increased basic benefits in low-benefit states, and permit eight or ten demonstration states to design and implement their own welfare programs for families with children.

H.R.4460 earned the support of all Republicans on the Ways and Means Committee and the Republican Research Committee, chaired by Congressmen Trent Lott (R-Miss.) and its Welfare Reform Task Force, chaired by Congressman Robert Walker (R-Pa.). On October 30, 1979, by a unanimous vote, including its chairman, Bud Shuster (R-Pa.), and Minority Leader John Rhodes (R-Ariz.), the House Republican Policy Committee voted to support H.R.4460 as "an initiative that provides true welfare reform" and to reject flatly the Carter-Kennedy-Corman proposal.

The goals of S. 1382 and H.R.4460 were to:

- Limit the growth of expenditures for the present open-ended federal family welfare program.
- Provide a strong incentive for the states to eliminate error, waste, and fraud in welfare programs and to reduce overall welfare spending.
- Provide all states with fiscal relief that may be used to reduce overall state welfare spending and to increase basic benefits for the truly needy.
- Encourage the states with the lowest per capita average income and lowest benefits to increase their basic family welfare benefit levels.
- Reverse the trend toward complete federalization of welfare by permitting eight or ten demonstration states to design and implement their own family welfare programs, tailored to meet the needs of the individual state and its poor. States would include a major industrial state, a rural state, and others drawn by lot from states whose governors have volunteered.
- Eliminate the need for a large federal bureaucracy to monitor the present open-ended federal matching system.
- Permit the states complete discretion to require work as a condition of eligibility for family welfare benefits.

- Reduce real federal spending for AFDC after five years by 2 percent per year to permit the federal budget to share the states' reductions in waste.

If the initial attempts succeed, the next step would be to permit all other states to join the eight or ten demonstration states in being free of all federal direction in designing and administering their family welfare programs. Later, federal block grants should be replaced by the states themselves after the federal government gives up some of its taxing authority.

This model for moving in an orderly manner in the AFDC program to return authority, responsibility, and tax resources to state governments should be used in other welfare programs such as Medicaid, housing, public service jobs, social services, and food stamps. If general conditions are imposed that require such funds, during their block grant status, to be used to provide health services, jobs, nutrition, and other assistance, it should be made clear that maximum authority and discretion be in the hands of the state and local governments.

I believe that the Reagan Administration, with Congressional support (augmented by the results of the 1980 election), will move in this new direction toward true welfare reform, which will relieve the taxpayer, reduce inflation, and provide necessary benefits to those genuinely in need.

9

THE REAGAN FOREIGN POLICY: AN OVERVIEW

GERALD HYMAN and
WAYNE VALIS

The foreign policy of the Reagan Administration will differ markedly from that of the Carter Administration. It will differ in policy, programs, and personnel, but, most vitally, in worldview and mind-set.

Explaining the difference in the *Washington Star*, a Reagan foreign policy adviser, Jeane J. Kirkpatrick, contends that "the most serious obstacles to an effective U.S. policy are, I believe, intellectual." Criticizing the recent foreign policy establishment, both "in and out of government," she described their mind-set as "long on wishes, ideology, and magical thinking. The wish is for world peace and an end to the arms race. The ideology is cosmopolitan and anti-anti-Communist. And the magic thinking consists of a conviction that we can control the world by our example."

Her "unsentimental appraisal," on the other hand, posits an expansionist Soviet Union possessing a "military establishment of unparalleled strength," freely using that strength in "coups, invasions, terrorism," and attempting to "replace autonomous governments with surrogate regimes." Professor Kirkpatrick notes some brutal facts: the efficacity of violence as "an instrument of political change, the vulnerability of less developed nations, the helplessness of the United Nations and the limited reliability of some of this country's . . . allies."

If Dr. Kirkpatrick is correct in her insistence that "the first step in an adequate response is intellectual . . . to learn again how to think realistically about our position in the world," then what will be the distinctive aspects of a Reagan foreign policy?

Perhaps the main foreign policy challenge confronting the U.S. during the next four years is to regain the confidence of its allies and the respect of potential adversaries. President Reagan faces the triple challenge of checking Soviet momentum, reversing Soviet gains where possible, and, above all, reasserting American leadership. For it should be clearly understood — and America must convey this understanding — that the clash between the Soviet Union and America is not a mere conflict of power like that, say, between nineteenth-century France and nineteenth-century Russia. It is more. It is a conflict between conceptions of human nature, ways of organizing society, beliefs about the rights of individuals and the appropriate powers of the state, and appropriate relations among nations. It is clear that the Reagan Administration will make these ideas part of the international debate and will guarantee that potential adversaries will not succeed in establishing their views by force.

Reagan Administration foreign policy spokesmen have asserted that the new government will concentrate on two areas: first, the formulation of a clear, principled, and consistent foreign policy, one characterized by coherence, realism, and reestablishment of a bipartisan approach; second, the development of economic and military strength, which will necessarily constitute the foundation of that policy.

With the highest trade deficit in our history, a 40 percent increase in our national debt, a 25 percent decline in the value of the dollar against the yen or the Deutsch mark, and the highest inflation rate since World War II, some analysts believe American economic strength has not been adequate to support our policy objectives, even had they been clear and consistent. And with a growing Soviet military capability in all areas — on land, sea, in the air, and in strategic weaponry — relative American capability to carry out its mission and to support U.S. foreign policy has been reduced.

During this Soviet buildup American military posture, or in President Reagan's words, our own "margin of safety," has deteriorated badly. The U.S. spends 5 percent of GNP on defense, compared with the Soviets' 10 percent. According to the Pentagon, six of our home-based Army divisions are not combat-ready; six of our thirteen carriers are not combat-ready. Some U.S. planes will not fly, our helicopters crash in the desert, and our Navy shipbuilding program has been reduced. The Commander of the U.S. Army in Europe says he has an "obsolete" army. The Chief of Naval Operations says he is asked to defend a three-ocean world with a one and a half ocean Navy. The Warsaw Pact outnumbers NATO by two and a half to one in tanks, over two to one in artillery, and nearly two to one in aircraft.

When President Carter declared the Soviet brigade in Cuba "unacceptable," later he had to accept it. He announced the "Carter Doctrine" — that the Persian Gulf was an area of vital interest to the West and, by implication, that any assault on the area or attempt to impede the free flow of oil would be repelled, by force if necessary — but later all but acknowledged he had no means to enforce it.

These objective difficulties were made worse by additional faulty perceptions and formulations. For example, the President toasted the Shah as "the island of stability in the Persian Gulf," then one year later waffled away our leverage with all factions in Iran — royal, military, moderate, and religious — unwittingly contributing to a radical rather than a moderate successor regime. He told us that we had an "inordinate fear of communism" and that he "held a deep belief that Brezhnev wants peace and friendship." After the invasion of Afghanistan, however, he discovered a different Brezhnev, one more consistent with those "inordinate" fears.

The task, as the new President has described it, is to reconstruct a more realistic, consistent, and convincing policy and rebuild the strength, both military and economic, to execute it. Reagan has said that the primary goal of his Administration will be "a lasting world peace, the restoration of American leadership as a force for freedom, for economic progress and for meeting basic human needs." Reagan recognizes that only restoration of U.S. military capability will provide the strength to keep the peace and dissuade Soviet adventurism.

The Reagan emphasis on restoration of the economy is designed, among other purposes, to assure the U.S. of the resources with which once again to fuel economic growth to help meet basic human needs. Those needs cannot be filled from an empty basket, and it is only in the Free World — Japan, Europe, North America — that the basket is growing. The Soviet bloc itself must borrow from the West. Poland alone owes the West $20 billion, of which $7 billion comes due shortly. Another $3.3 billion will be needed to finance the recent concessions to Poland's workers. It is the West that has the economic dynamics, and the West must use that strength to restore the balance.

Reagan's theme, "peace through strength," reflects his concern about the Soviet Union. While he seeks neither confrontation nor conflict, he is determined to protect U.S. interests through a realistic and balanced policy. He will attempt to negotiate with the Soviets to achieve real arms reduction, not a "freeze on Soviet superiority" or a "codified arms race." Reagan spokesmen have asserted the need for a comprehensive arms control strategy, designed to salvage what is useful of the SALT II proposals, yet at the same time turning its prime attention toward securing equitable, verifiable arms *reduction* as part of a SALT III treaty. The U.S. will attempt also to negotiate a Mutual Balanced Force Reduction (MBFR) that will truly be mutual and balanced and that will mean real reductions. The U.S. will seek to define areas of cooperation while both clearly asserting its interests and working toward peaceful means of competition where U.S. and Soviet interests diverge.

One of President Reagan's challenges will be to reverse the momentum of Soviet advances. U.S. security interests mandate steps to prevent potential Soviet domination of the sea-lanes in the Indian Ocean through basing or other new arrangements with allies and cooperative states in the region.

Proponents of an activist U.S. foreign policy contend that pressure can be indirectly applied on the Soviets so that they must bear an ever increasing cost for their Cuban proxies abroad. They also contend that direct or indirect assistance to help the Afghans secure again their independence and sovereignty, if properly directed, can impose severe costs on the Soviets.

President Reagan and his principal advisers have stated that the U.S. intends to link the desires of the Russians for trade and cooperation with their behavior elsewhere; the U.S. will measure their promises, for example at Helsinki, against their performance. The U.S. will signal to the Soviet leadership that many things are possible, many cooperations can be effected, but not if they are one-sided, or if the U.S. is expected to exercise all the restraint while the U.S.S.R. pursues all the gains.

President Reagan has indicated that he does not intend to act unilaterally. The U.S. will act in concert with our allies, from whom more will be asked, and of whom more will be expected. America's European allies want to reduce their dependence on the U.S., yet they are reluctant to expand their military or peacekeeping responsibilities. An America led by Ronald Reagan will exercise leadership, as Chancellor Schmidt recently called on America to do, but the allies will certainly be expected to lend substantial support.

One new avenue of allied cooperation may be in non-European areas of mutual and vital interest, areas like the Persian Gulf. The allies have quietly assembled a Western flotilla in the Gulf, and future additional steps may be taken as necessary. France's assumption, for instance, of responsibility to discourage Soviet-sponsored aggression in Africa could well serve as a model for other European initiatives.

The agenda for the NATO allies and Japan is long and complicated. For example, the new Administration will develop an integrated strategy for dealing with the deteriorating military balance, to revitalize the U.S. strategic deterrent, to modernize theater nuclear weapons and delineate doctrines to govern their use, to resolve NATO's "southern flank" issue (especially the Greek-Turkish conflict), to review nonproliferation policy, to develop comprehensive energy and strategic resource policies, and to work out long-range policies for processes of detente, MBFR, and SALT. All of these areas need to be discussed with our European allies.

In the Far East the U.S. confronts similar problems. U.S. relations with Japan remain rooted in postwar realities, despite radically changing newer realities. Japan is now the third most powerful economy in the world, and President Reagan must develop new modes for U.S.-Japanese interdependence.

Although the U.S. is expected to increase its military

capabilities and to deploy them in the Pacific and Indian Oceans, areas of vital concern to Japan, the Japanese spend less than 1 percent of their GNP on defense, compared with U.S. expenditures of over 5 percent. Clearly the burden of regional defense should be shared by those nations that can afford to do so and are its beneficiaries. While respecting the Japanese constitution and understanding Japanese sensitivity to any signs of "militarism," it is possible that nonmilitary financial adjustments may be requested by the President.

Regional defense was one impetus behind our new relationship with the People's Republic of China. The Reagan Administration will attempt to strengthen and extend that relationship, without losing sight of a commitment to safeguarding Taiwan's interests. Although the U.S. will welcome cooperation in areas of mutual interest (deterring Soviet expansion, for example), particularly in economic relations, the new Administration will do so with prudent caution for the strategic implications of high-technology transfers.

In the Middle East the Camp David process will be extended as long as it continues to appear fruitful. U.N. Resolutions 242 and 338 will serve as general principles for such a peace, which must be negotiated with the consent and participation of the major parties.

The petroleum-rich Middle East will remain a strategically important area of probable contention between the U.S.S.R. and the U.S. During the next decade, as the Soviet Union depletes its own easily available energy reserve, it will increasingly compete for Middle East resources. Although this competition will probably be peaceful, the U.S. must be prepared for the possibility that it may not be. Moreover, regional political volatility — local wars like that between Iran and Iraq or internal instability like that within Iran — poses a constant threat to a stable oil supply. The moderate Arab regimes in the Middle East look to the U.S. as a dependable, stable ally. President Reagan's Administration will no doubt give immediate attention to stabilizing the region.

Within our own region, close and friendly ties between the United States and other nations of the Hemisphere are a principal goal of a Reagan foreign policy. That policy, according to Administration spokesmen, will be built on a full understanding of the distinctive character of the various nations of the Hemisphere: the interests, problems, and needs of Brazil are different from those of Argentina, which are, in turn, different from those of Jamaica. Rather than a single Latin American policy, the Administration will pursue bilateral relations based on the distinct character of each of the parties.

Finally, both within the American Hemisphere and throughout the third world America is faced with one of the most intractable, yet potentially satisfying, of challenges: removing the yoke of hunger and poverty. Although many third world nations are now well on their way to fuller development, many, including some of the U.S.'s closest neighbors, are not. The U.S. will continue to assist these nations in a wide variety of ways, but the Administration will emphasize the export not only of our capital but of American know-how, technology, and marketing assistance as well. Equally important, the Reagan Administration will devote attention to convincing others, as we ourselves are convinced, of the superiority of free enterprise as the most effective means of eliminating poverty and preserving freedom as well.

In the end, that will be the major theme of the Reagan Administration. Attempting to reverse recent trends, it will work for peace, but only through the political, economic, and military strength that will insure peace with security. It will seek to extend freedom's mandate and to assure for our children and for those who have not yet tasted it that the liberty to which they are entitled will yet prevail.

10

THE FOREIGN AND DEFENSE POLICIES OF A REAGAN ADMINISTRATION

LAWRENCE J. KORB

The primary goal of the nation's foreign and defense policies is to provide for our national security and the protection of our interests. For purposes both of analysis and in actual practice, foreign and defense policy are often grouped together under the term "national security policy." Therefore, we refer to that body, which exists to coordinate and integrate the foreign or nonmilitary aspects with the defense or military components, as the National Security Council (NSC) and the decisions made by the NSC as national security policy.

This chapter, then, will focus on the national security policies likely to be pursued by the incoming Reagan Administration. Moreover, since the new President has indicated that he will place his main emphasis on the defense or military component, and since this is the area in which his policies will deviate most markedly from those of President Carter, the analysis will deal primarily with the defense policies of the new Administration.

DEFENSE POLICY

In the view of Reagan and his advisers, the fundamental
objective of U.S. defense policy is to deter an armed attack on the United States and its allies by a hostile
power by whatever means. And, if deterence fails, the
U.S. must have the military power to prevail in the ensu-
ing conflict with the minimum of damage to the lives
and property of our citizens or those of our allies.

Deterrence is accomplished by maintaining superiority or a margin of safety in the military balance vis-à-vis
one's enemies whether in the area of strategic or theater
nuclear forces or conventional forces. In the view of the
new President, the military forces of the U.S. are not
superior to those of our principal adversary, the Soviet
Union. On the contrary, primarily because of decisions
made by the Carter Administration, the military balance
now favors the U.S.S.R. across the board.

THE STRATEGIC NUCLEAR SITUATION

Reagan and his advisers accept the thesis that the U.S.
lost strategic parity in 1977, and we are now in a position of strategic inferiority. The data in Table 1 confirms
this view. As shown in the table, the Soviets now hold a
significant lead over the U.S. in four out of the five indicators of the strategic balance. The Russians now
have 500 more launchers or delivery vehicles. Their
forces possess almost twice as much throw-weight and
destructive power (EMT) and nearly three times as much
hard (military) target-kill potential. The only area in
which the U.S. has the edge is in the number of warheads. (For tables referred to see end of chapter.)

The new President is likewise alarmed about the
trends in the strategic balance. As Table 1 also shows,
given the current level of effort by the two superpowers
in the strategic area, the Soviets will be ahead of the U.S.
in every single indicator of the balance by 1985. And,
unless something is done quickly, the situation will con-

tinue to deteriorate through the remainder of the decade.

Ronald Reagan quite correctly perceives that maintenance of the strategic nuclear balance is critical. It is only the strategic nuclear forces of the Soviet Union that threaten the existence of our society and life as we know it. The rest of the world, allies as well as nonaligned countries, counts on the U.S. to maintain the strategic nuclear balance with the Soviet Union. If these nations detect a weakening in U.S. resolve to maintain the strategic umbrella, they will accommodate themselves to the dominant strategic power. Moreover, if this nation becomes a hostage to the strategic nuclear forces of the U.S.S.R., then it becomes difficult, if not impossible, for us to employ or risk using conventional force against Soviet interests, or to conduct its diplomacy successfully. Without strategic nuclear deterrence, the U.S. and its allies would always have the specter of Armageddon hanging over them.

Because of the importance of the strategic area, Reagan will no doubt move more rapidly in this area than his predecessor. President Reagan can be expected to undertake such steps as: accelerating the Trident submarine program, building a new-manned bomber, developing a new submarine-launched ballistic missile with hard target-kill capability (Trident II missile), and arming all 550 Minuteman III missiles with Mark 12-A warheads. Moreover, if the SALT process should collapse, a Reagan Administration would probably place Minuteman in a Multiple Protective Shelter (MPS) mode and deploy an antiballistic missile system.

Such programs would not only enhance deterrence by restoring the balance, but would also improve our nuclear war-fighting capabilities. Reagan supports Presidential Directive 59, which states that our nuclear forces must be capable of conducting a limited, as well as an all-out, nuclear attack and have a counterforce as well as a countervalue capability. However, the new President does not feel that we now have the forces to support that doctrine. For example, as Table 1 shows, we have only 800 weapons with hard target-kill capability. To support PD-59, we would need about 3,000. His new programs, plus the ongoing Carter programs, would give us that capability by the end of the decade.

THEATER NUCLEAR WEAPONS

The theater nuclear balance presents a picture similar to that of strategic nuclear weapons. As indicated in Table 2, in the European theater the theater nuclear forces (TNF) of the Warsaw Pact now have, and will continue to have, an increasing advantage over NATO in the area of theater nuclear weapons. The reasons for this situation are essentially the same as those that have created the strategic imbalance. While the Soviets have been deploying such TNF weapons as the SS-20 Mobile Intermediate Range Missile Bomber and the Backfire Bomber at the rate of five per week, the U.S. is still developing the Pershing 2 Ballistic Missile and the ground-launched Cruise Missile. While Reagan cannot affect the deployment rates of these weapons, now scheduled for the mid-1980s, he may initiate a program for placing land-attack Cruise Missiles on ships and submarines, reexamine Carter's decision not to deploy the neutron bomb, and use more strategic weapons in a theater role. He will not allow the TNF balance to remain as it is for too long, because this situation might tempt the Soviet Union to think that it could use or threaten to use these weapons without fear of reprisal.

CONVENTIONAL BALANCE

Our conventional or general purpose forces now exist to fight, along with our allies, a major war in Europe and a half, or minor, war outside Europe, most probably in the Persian Gulf area. This one and a half war doctrine will be accepted by the Reagan Administration. However, our force structure is lacking for each of those two contingencies. As Table 3 indicates, the U.S. and its NATO allies are outnumbered in people, hardware, and firepower by the Soviets and their allies. Moreover, although the manpower differential is relatively small, 13 percent, the weapons' gap is much greater. Table 3 shows that the Warsaw Pact has some 25,000 more tanks, planes, and artillery pieces than its NATO counterparts.

Our non-NATO force structure is not in much better shape. As Table 4 indicates, our Navy has declined by 50 percent, to 462 ships over the last decade, while the Soviet Navy has grown slightly. Compared with 1969, the U.S. Navy has significantly fewer ships in every category except nuclear-powered submarines, while the Soviets have added large numbers of surface combatants, nuclear submarines, and logistic ships. Though it might be going too far to say that the Soviet Navy is superior to ours, the fact is that they are a land-power basically self-sufficient in natural resources, whereas we are a maritime nation heavily dependent on other nations for resources. Therefore, we must control the seas to protect our national security and standard of living; they need not. The Soviets have merely to prevent us from doing so, a much less demanding task for a navy three times the size of ours.

Our flexible forces, for example, the Marines and some Army divisions, suffer from a severe lack of mobility. Using all of our airlift assets, it would take us two weeks to move one lightly armed division to the Persian Gulf and almost a month to place a fully mechanized division into the area. Placing a significant force of 200,000 men into the area would take a full six months!

This lack of conventional force structure is compounded by the inadequacies in our theater nuclear and strategic nuclear force postures discussed above. Since we dare not escalate the battle from the conventional to the nuclear, it is that much more important that our conventional forces be able to carry out their missions.

Obviously, force structure alone would not determine the outcome of a conventional battle. The side lacking the force structure can compensate for its force inadequacies by possessing more sustainability and being more ready. Unfortunately, our conventional forces have serious problems in each of these areas, which only compounds the problems created by an inadequate force structure.

All of our armed services lack sustainability, that is, the ability to carry on the battle for prolonged periods. If the Warsaw Pact launched a full-scale attack in Central Europe today, our Army would run short of skilled people, tanks, armored personnel, howitzers, artillery skills, tank rounds, mortar rounds, and bullets within twenty days. Moreover, given our lack of an industrial mobilization base, a combat-ready reserve force, and sealift capability, significant help from the continental U.S. would not begin arriving before ninety days. The Air Force in Europe is in equally poor condition. Its planes have enough missiles to fight for only two weeks. Overall, the Air Force has only one-third of its required inventory of missiles.

The Navy too has severe sustainability problems. It suffers from large shortages of torpedoes, missiles, and mines. Overall, it has only 50 percent of the ordnance it needs to conduct a war. Most of the forward deployed ships and planes would run out of ammunition after a few days of sustained combat. Similarly, the Marine Corps has far too few antitank weapons.

A force that is deficient in size and sustainability can often compensate for these problems through a high state of combat readiness — having the proper mix of men and equipment able to perform effectively at the initiation of hostilities. Historians generally agree that at the outbreak of World War II the Germans had fewer tanks and planes than the Allies but succeeded on the field because their forces had a higher state of readiness.

Our armed forces measure readiness on a unit basis by evaluating four areas. In each of these areas the unit commanding officer compares the unit's actual resources with those considered necessary to perform its wartime mission. The four areas that are evaluated are personnel, amount of equipment, quality of equipment, and training. On the basis of this evaluation, a unit is placed into one of five "C" categories.

C–1 Fully combat-ready.

C–2 Substantially combat-ready; that is, the unit has only minor deficiencies.

C–3 Marginally combat-ready; that is, the unit has major deficiencies but can still perform its assigned missions.

C–4 Not combat-ready because the unit has so many deficiencies that it cannot perform its wartime functions.

C–5 Not combat-ready because the unit is undergoing a planned period of overhaul or maintenance. For example, the carrier *Saratoga* is in the Philadelphia Naval yard having its service life extended by fifteen years.

(The difference between C-4 and C-5 is that a unit in the latter group is undergoing routine or planned maintenance, while the C-4 unit breaks down unexpectedly or at a time when it is supposed to be in a state of good repair.)

Table 5 breaks down the current operational readiness of our conventional forces by service. Overall, except for the Marine Corps, none of the services is in very good shape. The Navy and Army are experiencing the most readiness problems. Only 31 percent of the Navy's ships and combat aircraft do not have serious inadequacies.

Some 36 percent are not combat-ready, while another 33 percent are combat-ready but have major problems. The situation in the Navy has become so bad that it is routinely deploying C-4 ships and last spring actually had to tie up a ship because of personnel shortages. Similarly, only six of the Army's sixteen divisions are without major difficulties. Although the Air Force may not be in as poor condition as the Army and Navy, it still has more than 40 percent of its units with serious deficiencies. Moreover, while the Marine Corps is currently reporting that all of its divisions and air squadrons are combat-ready, one must remember that the Marine Corps has been "C-2 for 200 years." Therefore, one must take such reports with a degree of skepticism.

The present readiness problems of our armed services are chiefly personnel-related: units unable to fulfill combat functions. There is both a quantitative and qualitative shortfall in our armed forces. Overall, the military services have dropped from 2.3 million people in 1973 to about 2 million at present, because they have been unable to meet their recruiting and retention goals. For example, last year the armed forces missed their recruiting goal by 8 percent and their retention objective by 9 percent. The services also lack some 70,000 skilled noncommissioned or petty officers, the middle managers who possess the critical skills and experience to see that the essential tasks of military units are performed. Finally, there is a shortage of 10,000 middle-grade officers. This shortage is concentrated primarily among officers who are pilots, engineers, and doctors.

Moreover, there are severe qualitative problems among those who are recruited and are being retained by the services. For example, in the first three quarters of FY 1980, only 38 percent of the people joining the Army had a high-school diploma while 45 percent of those who joined in FY 1979 were classified in mental category IV. The result of the Army's 1979 skill qualifications tests were horrendous. Overall, about half of the soldiers taking different job skill tests failed to pass. In ten skill rates the failure rate was over 90 percent. For example, 98 percent of tank repairmen failed; as did 91 percent of the aviation maintenance personnel; 86 percent of artillery crewmen; 83 percent of transportation personnel; 69 percent of the communications people; 51 percent of the military intelligence personnel; 49 percent of the combat engineers; and 43 percent of the field artillerymen. Only three bassoon players, eleven special agents, and sixteen missile mechanics were able to constitute skill groups passing their tests by 100 percent.

The reasons for these personnel and readiness problems are understood by the Reagan Administration. We, as a society, have not kept faith with those whom we have asked, or will ask, to join the volunteer military. We have not kept our commitment to maintain the competitiveness of military pay. Compared with 1972, when we inaugurated the All-Volunteer Force (AVF), military pay has fallen nearly 20 percentage points relative to the Consumer Price Index (CPI). Moreover, compared with the pay of blue-collar workers and unionized workers, groups with whom the military must compete for skilled people, the pay of the armed services has fallen by some 25 percentage points. The compensation situation has gotten so bad that thousands of military people are paid less than the minimum wage and are eligible for food stamps. In addition, we have allowed housing allowances, moving expenses, and medical benefits programs to fall so far behind their actual costs that many service people are digging into their own pockets for thousands of dollars to pay for these items. Finally, we have constantly threatened, almost on a routine basis, to change the retirement system and abolish such "fringe" benefits as commissaries and exchanges. It is no wonder that highly qualified people are not attracted to join or stay in today's armed forces, or that those who remain have low morale.

Moreover, under the programs of the Carter Administration the force imbalances and readiness problems will continue to get worse. We not only have underfunded investment over the past two decades, but will not close the gap with the Soviets in the next five years. It is unlikely that a Reagan Administration will allow the force structure imbalances or readiness and sustainability problems to persist very long. We can expect to see it embark quickly on a vigorous program of force modernization, as well as a program of making our current force structure well, that is, of improving its readiness.

Additional modernized forces will probably go first into our flexible forces, primarily the Navy and Marine Corps. We can expect to see a shipbuilding program that will build at least twenty ships a year in contrast to the present level of fifteen and more emphasis on providing lift for the Marine Corps and "light" Army forces. In addition, the Army and Air Force annual weapons procurement totals will increase as the Reagan Administration moves toward more efficient procurement policies. This will not only increase our weapons inventory more rapidly but will also save money in the long run.

The readiness situation will be attacked primarily by curing the problem of recruiting and retaining qualified people. Since Reagan is committed to giving the All-Volunteer Force the fair chance that it has never received, we can expect President Reagan to move swiftly to restore comparability in military pay by enacting across-the-board real increases and to enhance competitiveness by providing substantial bonuses for those officers and noncommissioned officers with special and critical skills. A secondary emphasis will be on procuring larger quantities of items like spare parts and consumables (ammunition, missiles, torpedoes). These items, which do not have as big a constituency as large weapon systems like ships and tanks, have a direct impact on readiness and have been seriously underfunded in recent years.

THE PACE OF IMPROVEMENT
How quickly the Reagan Administration can restore the military balance across the board will depend upon how much money can be made available to defense and how quickly defense can absorb the additional funds. For FY 1981 defense spending will amount to about $154 billion. This will equal 5.5 percent of GNP and 24 percent of the appropriated federal budget.

Building from this base, it would be difficult to raise defense outlays much above 6 percent of the GNP before FY 1984. If Reagan does this, the defense budget would rise to $240 billion, or 25 percent of the federal budget in FY 1984. This would represent a real increase of about 5 percent per year over the next three years and would allow the President to make great improvements in the readiness area. Dramatic changes in the force balances would have to be made in the post-FY 1984 period unless defense receives about 7 percent of the GNP and 30 percent of the federal budget. However, even 6 percent might be difficult if the President wishes to balance the budget and reduce taxes simultaneously.

FOREIGN POLICY
While the United States is raising its defense expenditures and thus increasing its military capabilities, a Reagan Administration can be expected to put pressure on our allies to do the same. It will be forced to do this both for practical and political reasons. The U.S. can no longer bear the burden of defense alone. Nor will a Congress support an increased effort by the U.S. not matched by our allies, who benefit from our efforts and are economically more capable than we to increase spending.

If Reagan could convince the NATO countries and Japan to put 5 percent of their GNP into defense, the free world could add $60 billion in additional funds for defense in FY 1981. In addition to asking them to raise their defense expenditures, the new Administration will also put pressure on our allies to provide offsets for the

American presence in Europe, the Persian Gulf, and Western Pacific, and to purchase more military hardware from us.

The skill with which these issues are handled will have a great impact on the ability of the U.S. to reassume its leadership role in the alliance. Moreover, if the U.S. and its allies build up their defense capability sufficiently, they will be able to negotiate with the Soviet Union from the preferred position of the Reagan Administration, that is, a position of strength.

This will be the key to American foreign policy in the Reagan Administration. The new President sees the Soviet Union as the underlying cause of most of the national security problems confronting the United States. If the allied buildup moderates Soviet behavior, the national security policies of the new Administration will be a success. If it does not, our security and that of the rest of the world will be jeopardized. The decade of the 1980s promises to be chaotic enough without the additional pressures of U.S.-Soviet acrimony.

TABLE 1

Strategic Forces of the U.S. and U.S.S.R. for Selected Calendar Years

	1980		1985		1990	
Category	U.S.	U.S.S.R.	U.S.	U.S.S.R.	U.S.	U.S.S.R.
Delivery vehicles						
ICBMs	1,054	1,398	1,054	1,238–1,400	900	1,238–1,500
SLBMs	656	950	688	900–1,000	720	900–1,100
Penetrating bombers[a]	348	156	220	100–200	180	100–200
ALCM bombers	––	––	100	––	150	25–50
Total vehicles	2,058	2,504	2,062	2,238–2,600	1,950	2,263–2,850
Warheads[b]	9,200	6,000	10,300	9,400–11,000	12,800	9,500–12,500
Total throw-weight[c]	6,800	11,000	7,700	13,500–15,000	8,946	14,500–15,000
EMT[d]	3,300	5,500	4,000	6,800–8,000	4,633	8,000–8,700
Hard target kill potential	800	2,000	900	500–5,200	2,000	6,500–6,800

Dash (––) = Nil.
[a] Excludes U.S. FB-111 and Soviet Backfire.
[b] Independently targetable weapons.
[c] In thousands of pounds.
[d] Equivalent megatonnage, a measure of destructive power based upon both yield and accuracy.
SOURCES: International Institute for Strategic Studies, *The Military Balance, 1979-80*, pp. 86-88; and *FY 1981 Defense Report*, pp. 71, 87, 89, and 123-35.

TABLE 2

Long-Range Theater Nuclear Balance,
FY 1980-1990

Category	1980 NATO	1980 Warsaw Pact	1985 NATO	1985 Warsaw Pact	1990 NATO	1990 Warsaw Pact
Delivery vehicles[a]	226	900	435	1,250	740	1,500
Warheads	500	2,100	775	3,250	925	3,880
EMT	1:3	3:1	1:4	4:1	1:4	4:1
Hard target kill potential	1:1	1:1	1:2	2:1	1:2	2:1

[a] Includes only land-based missiles and aircraft based in Europe.
SOURCES: Derived from *FY 1981 Defense Report,* pp. 93 and 145-49; *The Military Balance, 1979-80,* pp. 114-19; and Justin Galen, "Can NATO Meet Its Toughest Test?" *Armed Forces Journal,* November 1979, p. 52.

TABLE 3

Balance of Forces in Europe in 1979

Category	NATO	Warsaw Pact	Warsaw Pact Advantage Amt.	Warsaw Pact Advantage (%)
Ground troops	1,176,000	1,331,000	155,000	(13)
Tanks	11,000	27,200	16,200	(147)
Tactical aircraft	3,300	5,795	2,495	(76)
Artillery pieces	6,200	14,000	7,800	(126)

SOURCE: Derived from *The Military Balance, 1979-80,* pp. 3-30 and 108-13.

TABLE 4

Active Naval Forces of the U.S. and U.S.S.R., 1969-1979

Ship Type	1969		1979[a]		Change, 1969-1979	
	U.S.	U.S.S.R.	U.S.	U.S.S.R.	U.S.	U.S.S.R.
Aircraft carriers	22	—	13	2	−9	2
Surface combatants	279	220	178	269	−101	49
Nuclear submarines	79	63	118	142	39	79
Conventional submarines	77	291	5	215	−72	−76
Patrol combatants	9	148	3	120	−6	−28
Amphibious	153	103	63	91	−90	−12
Mine warfare	74	165	3	165	−71	0
Mobile logistic	112	56	59	150	−53	94
Support	119	624	20	610	−99	−14
Total	924	1,670	462	1,764	−462	94

Dash (—) = Nil.

[a] As of December 1979.

SOURCE: *Statement of Admiral Thomas B. Hayward on the FY 1981 Military Posture and FY 1981 Budget, February 7, 1979,* p. 51.

TABLE 5
Readiness of Units by Service in Mid–1980
(in Percentages)

Readiness Category

	C-1	C-2	C-3	C-4	C-5	Percentage of DOD Units Reporting
Army	–	37	25	38	–	3
Navy	3	28	33	15	21	76
Air Force	18	39	18	16	9	18
Marine Corps	–	70	30	–	–	3
Total	6	32	30	15	17	100

SOURCE: Author's Estimates

11

NATIONAL DEFENSE: THE STRATEGIC FRAMEWORK

DANIEL O. GRAHAM

The Reagan Administration faces huge but not insurmountable problems in the area of national defense. President Reagan inherits the results of fifteen years of adherence to faulty strategic concepts — notably the Mutual Assured Destruction doctrine — and ten years of highly destructive assaults on the U.S. military and intelligence structures, assaults that became politically fashionable toward the end of the Vietnam War and remained so until recently.

A dangerous debilitation of U.S. military and intelligence capabilities had occurred even before the advent of the Carter Administration, but were sharply accelerated over the past four years. The Carter Administration hierarchy, in the national security "cluster" especially, was staffed with true believers in the virtues of unilateral disarmament and dismantlement of U.S. defense commitments abroad. As a result, military programs that were favorite targets of anti-defense lobbies were summarily axed. After an abortive try (in March 1977) to secure a SALT agreement that might have provided some braking of the Soviet nuclear buildup, the Carter Administration promptly negotiated SALT II, which so readily capitulated to Soviet demands that it could not be ratified by an awakening U.S. Senate.

One of the more disturbing legacies of the Carter Administration is a seriously politicized military establishment. Early on, the Carter Administration made it clear that the leadership of the U.S. military had no option but to support any and all decisions of the new team. Through reprimands and dismissal from posts, it soon became evident that the military was not merely to remain silent when policies and actions ran counter to their professional judgment, but that voluble *support* was a prerequisite to retention of position. Thus, the capabilities of the U.S. defense establishment were perilously weakened, and the institutions that should be relied upon to provide the professional advice on how to repair the damage have been grievously impaired.

A brief status report on the various elements of the national defense structure follows.

THE STRATEGIC NUCLEAR BALANCE

The balance is bad, the trends are worse. The Russians have the U.S. outnumbered in intercontinental missilery, land and sea-based, by 50 percent. We continue to hold an edge in intercontinental bombers only when one accepts the dangerous assumption that the newest Soviet strategic bomber (Backfire) would never be used against the U.S. despite its obvious capabilities for intercontinental attack. The Russians' less-than-intercontinental range bombers and missiles outnumber the Europeans' nuclear force over five to one. The technical edge once enjoyed by the U.S. has been reduced by the U.S.S.R. to near insignificance. For instance, there is no longer a meaningful difference between U.S. and Soviet missile accuracy.

The strategic offensive imbalance in favor of the U.S.S.R. is bad enough, but the imbalance in strategic *defenses* is even worse. The United States has almost no strategic defense, while the Soviet Union has massive antibomber and antimissile defenses, plus a well-developed civil defense. The combination of superior strategic nuclear offensive power and overwhelming advantages in nuclear defenses account for one estimate that the U.S. would lose 140 to 160 million citizens as the immediate result of a nuclear exchange, the U.S.S.R. as few as 10 million. This awesome disparity drastically impairs the effectiveness of the U.S. deterrent to nuclear war and increases the willingness of the U.S.S.R. to present the West with military confrontations. Unless corrected, the strategic nuclear imbalance will continue to increase the likelihood of major war.

ARMS CONTROL
The SALT process is in serious jeopardy — not because "hawks" have attacked SALT II, but because overly enthusiastic proponents of arms control have negotiated and supported a treaty so inequitable and flawed that it could not pass muster in the Senate. If, as supporters of the treaty have insisted, SALT II is the best we can hope to get, it follows that the arms-control process is at a hopeless impasse.

CONVENTIONAL FORCES
Those U.S. and allied military forces maintained to deter or, if deterrence fails, to conduct nonnuclear theater warfare are not now, and never have been, adequate to deter or defeat an all-out conventional assault by the U.S.S.R. and its allies. The efficacy of our conventional forces in this role has always depended in part on superior tactical nuclear forces and, beyond them, superior strategic nuclear forces. The inevitable corollary to the assumption that nuclear war is so destructive

as to be unthinkable is the assumption that *any* major war between the superpowers is next to unthinkable because such a conflict would almost certainly escalate to nuclear war. Thus, the doctrines of Mutual Assured Destruction, which led to neglect of the strategic balance, have led to neglect of conventional balance as well.

Neglect of conventional theater forces has resulted in shortages of first-line equipment, inadequate munitions and spare parts stocks, and depletion of the Reserves and National Guard. What is worse, the potential of such conventional forces as *are* available has been greatly eroded by shortages of qualified personnel. Six of our first-line Army divisions are unfit for combat, several Navy ships have been unable to put to sea for lack of qualified sailors, and Air Force planes are grounded in unacceptable proportions for lack of qualified maintenance personnel.

MILITARY PERSONNEL

A persistant squeeze on pay and allowances, coupled with a general weakening of esprit de corps in the military services, has seriously affected the competence of the forces. Low pay relative to comparable civilian jobs has resulted in a steady drain of highly qualified people from the military to the civilian sector.

A second problem arises from the low-quality input at the bottom of the military ladder. The All-Volunteer Force concept has worked badly thus far. The recruiting services, attempting to meet numerical quotas, enlist misfits and untrainables. More than 40 percent of newly enlisted personnel never complete their first year of military service. Of those retained beyond a year a high percentage are functional illiterates. Such results are a gross waste of defense dollars and incompatible with the increasing technical complexity of military equipment.

INTELLIGENCE

In all three of the prime functions of intelligence the

United States is now dangerously deficient. One prime function is the provision of reliable information to the executive branch and the Congress on which to base foreign policy and security decisions; another is the protection of legitimate state secrets; the third is the conduct of covert action in support of U.S. foreign policy. All U.S. intelligence functions are suffering from an excessive reaction to the allegations of "abuse" in the post-Watergate mid-seventies. Some of the unnecessary restriction is in the form of unsound legislation (e.g., the Freedom of Information Act), some in the form of executive orders.

Some of the serious problems afflicting our intelligence effort are of long standing. They result from the impracticality of attempting to give central authority over major portions of the Departments of Defense and State to a sub-Cabinet level agency, the CIA. This arrangement engenders fierce, destructive, and essentially insoluble parochial rivalries. Attempts to produce a single, "coordinated" answer to key intelligence questions produce homogenized intelligence judgments damping out important analytical differences among competent intelligence analysts.

MILITARY ESTABLISHMENT STRUCTURE

The Joint Chiefs of Staff structure, as created by the National Security Act of 1947, is no longer an adequate mechanism for the provision of professional military advice to the President and the Congress. The Chiefs, as individuals, are captives of their individual services' major hardware programs, most of which they inherited from predecessors. Collectively, they have been professionally compromised by an inability to resist purely political pressures from a sitting Administration. Internally, the JCS has been reduced to the role of occasional plaintiff against decisions of a massive civilian DOD bureaucracy.

The Pentagon today is characterized by legions of

civilian and military bureaucrats organized and engaged in the process of offsetting one another in interdepartmental matters.

THE REAGAN OPTIONS

Only a President with a strong mandate for change in the foreign affairs/national security area could make the bold changes necessary to correct the sad state of affairs briefly outlined above. Fortunately, the Reagan Administration has such a mandate. An informed public is generally demanding of improved security; the House and Senate are for the first time in decades prepared to support vigorous action to improve national security. Thus President Reagan should have a good chance of correcting national security shortcomings and even introducing sweeping changes provided his programs show cohesion and costs are within the realm of reason.

The Reagan advisory groups on foreign affairs and on national security concluded that in general the cluster of security problems should be approached as follows:

- First, establish a framework of U.S. strategy.
- Second, determine the military capabilities required to support that strategy.
- Third, initiate or reemphasize military programs designed to provide those capabilities, rejecting or deemphasizing programs that do not contribute to end goals.
- Fourth, restructure the establishment as required to insure efficient execution.

Each of these steps can be addressed in two essentially different modes: bold change or incremental adjustment. For instance, the serious problem of the unfavorable strategic nuclear balance can be addressed by the bold change to a new technology that shows promise of "end-running" the current Soviet numerical advantages, or, incrementally, by adjusting U.S. programs in such a way as to close that numerical gap. While bold changes have an immediate appeal in most cases, they usually require more time than incremental changes — perhaps too much time. Thus, most answers tend to evolve into combinations of bold change and incremental adjustment.

OVERALL STRATEGY

This is the most Presidential of decisions to be made: What in fact shall be our national strategy? Further, the enunciation of a strategic framework is absolutely essential to an effective and coordinated effort by all elements of the foreign policy/national security/intelligence cluster of government.

Clearly the set of doctrines of the past fifteen years (which have not in fact constituted a strategy) have proved unsatisfactory at best, disastrous at worst. These doctrines are those generally contained under the rubrics of detente and disarmament. I will not attempt in this short paper a thoroughgoing definition of a "Reagan era strategy." Suffice it to say that the Reagan strategy will more closely resemble the containment strategy of the Truman, Eisenhower, Kennedy years than it will the detente srategy of the Johnson, Nixon, Ford, Carter years. The long-term goal will be to produce a world environment in which free political and economic systems flourish in security as totalitarian systems wither under the weight of their own unjustices and ineptitude — *and* to achieve that goal while avoiding a major armed clash of competing systems. This requires that the armed forces of the United States, in combination with those of its Free World allies, shall be adequate to deter aggression at the higher scales of violence and cope with aggression at the lower scales of violence. Therein lies the prime imperative for addressing U.S. national security problems.

STRATEGIC FORCES

The immediate problem facing the United States in the

area of strategic forces is the universally accepted estimate that the U.S.S.R. will, toward the end of Mr. Reagan's term, be able to destroy the major part of the U.S. deterrent force before it is launched. This is not to say an attack will then ensue, but that the once-unchallenged U.S. deterrent will have little effect on the audacity of Russian actions at other levels of un-pleasantness. This situation has been brought about by an inexorable buildup of highly effective Soviet inter-continental ballistic missiles. This would permit them to strike our deterrent force with less than a quarter of their intercontinental arsenal, leaving the remainder to threaten the wholescale slaughter of our population should we be foolish enough not to admit defeat after the first disarming strike by Soviet forces.

The Carter Administration addressed this bleak situation with a proposal for a new missile, MX, deployed in such a fashion that no additional U.S. strength would be available before 1986, with a maximum of 200 new missiles by 1990 — all at tremendous cost. But Carter was saddled with a dedication to MAD doctrines, and such systems as MX Racetrack were designed to be compatible with SALT II. Reagan is not thus encumbered and has more effective options.

One such option is to end-run the Soviet massive buildup technologically by deploying space-borne defenses that could negate the Soviet threat to our deterrent forces. A partial space-borne defense against a Soviet first strike could, with sufficient emphasis, be placed on line quicker than the first MX missile could be. Even more quickly, some of the cheaper defensive systems developed by the Army could be installed to protect, at least in part, currently deployed U.S. strategic missiles. These options, cheaper and more effective than current programs, require rejection of current MAD doctrines, which hold strategic defenses to be provoc-ative — except, strangely enough, those pursued by the Soviet Union.

This is but one example of the bold changes based on advanced technology that are possible. But some of the incremental approach would be required as well. For instance, the B-1 bomber program should be reinstituted so that our SAC bomber force becomes somewhat less vulnerable. Also, some rebasing may be required if the overall threat to the bomber on the ground is not correctable in time by strategic defenses. Further, it may be necessary to restart the Minuteman III missile production line to offset delays in the availability of MX.

CONVENTIONAL FORCES
Probably the most fundamental change in the conventional ground forces would evolve from a strategic decision to divide responsibilities with our allies. Conventional strength along static lines of confrontation — in Central Europe, for instance — should be the primary responsibility of the allies whose territory is most affected. The United States should shift its attention in conventional capabilities to the more indirect threats to the total Alliance, among them the threat to the Middle East. In both cases U.S. and allied participation should be on a scale adequate to insure the solidarity of the Alliance. That is to say, some U.S. forces should remain in Europe and some European forces should be assigned to an allied Middle East Task Force.

The Rapid Deployment Force that has been much heralded of late should probably become either the U.S. Marine Corps or an Army Airborne Corps.

Much of the repair of our conventional capabilities comes in more prosaic incremental packages. We can expect an early Reagan Administration effort to correct pay discrepancies, replenish basic stocks of spare parts and munitions, and speed delivery of new equipment.

ARMS LIMITATION
The Reagan approach to SALT has already been fairly well spelled out. SALT II will not be ratified. Negotiations

will be offered on a more comprehensive SALT III. One would not expect a Reagan SALT negotiating team to fall into the traps of the past, however. There will probably be no public description of tough terms à la Jimmy Carter in March 1977, nor an overweening, politically in-spired urge to show "progress" in SALT that led Carter and his predecessors to accept bad terms. SALT has lost its savor with most Americans, and the Reagan Ad-ministration owes nothing to the remaining proponents of agreement for agreement's sake.

INTELLIGENCE

The Central Intelligence Agency will probably lose some of its preeminence in intelligence matters. Most Reagan advisers agree that there should be more than one source of wisdom on key intelligence issues. Thus, the process whereby CIA blended all views into an estimate representing the director's view, and other views were relegated to the position of a dissent, will almost cer-tainly be altered.

On the other hand, the primacy and emphasis of CIA on clandestine services will probably increase. Some Reagan advisers are convinced that clandestine ser-vices should be separated from CIA's analysis functions. Others argue (I among them) that this is not a wise move, as it makes clandestine collection and encour-ages the show-and-tell urge of collectors — the urge to run to high officials with raw, uncollated reports.

The initials CIA may in fact disappear in favor of some such name as the Foreign Intelligence Service. Such a change would be more than merely cosmetic, for it would mark a change from the concept that all intelli-gence can in fact be centralized and that the Agency is somehow responsible for domestic as well as foreign in-telligence.

THE NATIONAL SECURITY STRUCTURE

Among Reagan advisers serious consideration is probably being given to proposing to the Congress a National Security Act of 1981 to replace the Act of 1947. Some of the more sweeping proposed changes to the intelligence structure, to the Defense Department, and to the National Security Council suggest such a new act. A new act could create a more rational policy-decision structure, restore a workable channel for professional military advice to political leadership, and remove the rationale for cumbersome bureaucracy.

MILITARY PERSONNEL

Reagan has expressed his opposition to a peacetime draft. It is no secret, however, that many of his advisers disagree on this point. At this juncture a thoroughgoing effort to make the All-Volunteer system succeed seems likely to precede any movement by the Reagan Administration toward a draft.

Measures to make All-Volunteer work will certainly include pay incentives to highly skilled personnel, stricter rules for recruiters, and perhaps a program to purge the forces of their lowest-caliber people. If this can be done without a drastic reduction in numbers, the All-Volunteer system may survive. If not, a Reagan Administration could be forced to reinstitute a draft of some sort.

CONCLUSION

In sum, we can expect a Reagan Administration to chart bold, realistic new courses in national strategy and programs to support that strategy. "Quick fixes" and incremental adjustments to ongoing programs will be designed to move the defense establishment in the direction of the more fundamental changes required. We can also expect reforms of the national security establishment to streamline the decision-making process.

12

MIDDLE EAST CHALLENGES

DALE R. TAHTINEN

The Middle East is a highly critical region for the United States for several reasons. The most immediately important aspect of the region lies in the fact that the Persian Gulf countries alone account for some 50 percent of all oil exports and about 45 percent of proven reserves worldwide. Furthermore, the greatest likelihood of new discoveries being made in large quantities leans strongly toward the probability that such finds will occur in countries bordering the Persian Gulf.

Another important element of the Middle East relative to American foreign policy lies in the fact that the geostrategic location of the region is crucial to NATO's southern flank. It is one thing to have basically neutral countries or even somewhat anti-American states along the southern and eastern tiers of the Mediterranean, but it would create a significantly greater magnitude of concern if more Qaddafi-type regimes began to appear in just those states littoral to that body of water.

Also, within the Middle East region exists a nation the United States is morally and ethically committed to defend. The challenge of creating a more peaceful climate for the Israeli nation will be a major element of the

148

Reagan Administration's foreign policy in that area.

Protecting Israel requires the support of a powerful and generally economically independent United States. There is little doubt that, based upon over two hundred years of rich history, this country has established its credentials as a just and peace-loving nation. In that regard, there is no other comparable nation on earth to challenge our position effectively.

Yet, as the annals of history also record, culturally rich and diverse nations have had great difficulty surviving without such military strength that they are never forced to capitulate in the face of superior force. Unfortunately, in the Middle East the United States is presently confronted by awesome challenges to its once dominant military capabilities. Thus, serious questions must be answered about this nation's ability to defend adequately the interests of those countries deemed crucial by Washington.

The Reagan Administration will undoubtedly place its support squarely behind Israel with all the power at its disposal. Indeed, Mr. Reagan has stated that Israel is not only a nation, it is a symbol. During the campaign he emphasized how Israel symbolizes the values of family, work, neighborhood, peace, and freedom so cherished by Americans. When we are defending Israel's right to exist, Reagan contends, we are defending the very values upon which American society is built.

To defend the Israeli nation effectively, however, requires more than a moral commitment and strikes at the very heart of the American quandary in the Middle East. The military power necessary to protect an ally like Israel necessitates the availability of large-scale military force for possible use in times of crisis. Yet equally important is the essential need for military power that can be projected anywhere else in the world where the Soviet Union or other belligerents might simultaneously challenge the security interests of the United States.

Consequently, this country cannot afford to be the number two power in the world.

In apparent recognition of the difficulties facing what has been an erosion of American military power worldwide, Reagan was quick to indicate that the commitment to Israel requires a globally strong America, whose strength is based upon a powerful economy. In a most appropriate statement, Reagan, as candidate, pointed out that no single policy, "no matter how deeply rooted in the humanitarian vision we share, can succeed if the United States of America continues its descent into economic impotence and despair."

Yet the cruel predicament confronting the Reagan Administration is that the massively powerful economy so essential for the United States is highly vulnerable to the availability of petroleum from the Arab oil producers, especially the Persian Gulf states. At a minimum, this situation will continue to be present, at least in the short run. Indeed, even with the immediate lifting of regulations on domestic pricing and massive investment for internal production, combined with an aggressive energy alternatives program, the United States will still be importing a significant quantity of petroleum during the decade of the 1980s.

Consequently, the Reagan Administration will be constantly dealing with the seemingly intractable problem of protecting Israel while relying on Arab oil. At any juncture it is possible that the Arabs may initiate some type of oil embargo if they perceive that the United States is not doing enough to solve the thorny Palestinian question, as well as other highly sensitive issues of a territorial nature, such as future control of Jerusalem and the Golan Heights.

The Reagan Administration can be expected to continue being sympathetic toward Israel positions regarding Jerusalem and the Palestine Liberation Organization (PLO). Mr. Reagan has made it quite clear that the United

States should not attempt to dissuade other nations from setting up their embassies in Jerusalem, and said he had no hesitation in branding the PLO as a terrorist organization. With respect to the PLO, Mr. Reagan said he feels it must renounce its charter calling for the destruction of Israel and become truly representative of the Palestinian people if it is to be a legitimate representative body. He is also emphatic that Israel should not have a radical Palestinian state on its border.

In attempting to resolve the Palestinian issue, the Reagan Administration will undoubtedly expend considerable effort on seeking a solution via the Jordanians. Consequently, King Hussein will likely become a leader of crucial importance.

Should attempts at peacemaking fail and large-scale hostilities erupt, it is possible that a new oil embargo may be set in motion by the Arab states. If that occurs, the United States will be caught in a serious dilemma. Efforts might be made to seize the oil fields, which could easily lead to an extended cutoff of oil because of military actions and sabotage, throwing the West into a desperate economic situation. On the other hand, there might be a genuine fear that to do nothing could lead to a perception of American weakness in confronting a challenge to the national interest of the United States.

Consequently, a very early effort in the Reagan Administration will be to improve and expand American military capability in critical areas of the world, particularly in the Middle East. Considerable effort and resources expended upon a rapid deployment force capability and naval task forces will most likely receive increasingly greater attention.

More specifically, Israel will continue to receive extensive assistance in the economic and military arenas, and close cooperation can be even expected to increase between that nation and the United States. The Reagan Administration will almost certainly consider Israel a strategic asset, and the Israelis will be expected to occupy a strong role in fighting Communist influence in the area.

Indeed, one of the hallmarks of the Reagan Administration can be expected to entail a sizable effort to prevent Soviet gains in the region. There will be a keen recognition and appreciation of Soviet motives in the area and a special sensitivity regarding any American action that might be perceived as a sign of weakness.

Moscow will undoubtedly do a lot of probing, confronting the Reagan Administration with some provocative challenges in this crucial region. The difficulties that might face the new American government are particularly intriguing because the Russians are in a unique situation to create trouble, and, if the past is any criterion, will not hesitate to avail themselves of the opportunities.

First, in terms of the oil-producing states of the Persian Gulf, the Soviets could undertake actions that might negatively affect the flow of oil destined directly for Western countries. This could be done by indirectly sponsoring insurgents to operate against the more conservative regimes, fanning the fires of local conflicts between existing governments or attempting to drive a wedge between the policies of Western nations and the United States.

In the latter attempt, the Palestinian issue may provide the very opportunity Moscow seeks for its goals. The Russians could encourage and support all efforts aimed at a European initiative regarding a Palestinian state. They could then offer protection to the oil-producing states by guaranteeing them protection against American military action if the producers applied a selective embargo against the United States because it failed to support the European initiative. In such a situation the Russians could conceivably befriend the producers as well as the Western consumers, except for the United States and possibly a few other countries.

More direct, but still short of actual seizure, would be to extend the existing Soviet Union/Eastern European pipeline network to the Gulf and provide a security guarantee for the route. Such an arrangement would obviously have considerable economic benefit for Moscow. Of even greater importance, however, would be the political control the socialist countries would have affecting Western European energy supplies, which would daily traverse socialist territory.

Ultimately, of course, there is always the lurking possibility that the Kremlin might choose to dispatch troops directly into the region to protect a "friendly" regime that requests assistance, as they contend occurred in Afghanistan. The Russians may also be preparing to support certain secessionist movements with much greater direct assistance, an action that could have considerable impact in such nearby states as Pakistan, Iran, and even Iraq or Turkey. The Reagan Administration will be preparing for such a series of contingencies, particularly in light of the Afghanistan invasion and the historic Russian desire for a warm water port.

Indeed, brief examination of some of the more sizable ethnic groups in the northern tier countries reveals considerable potential for Soviet-sponsored troublemaking. To the east of Afghanistan lies the Northwest Frontier District of Pakistan, where some eight million Pushtuns live, often under fragile Pakistan control, while in pre-invasion Afghanistan some forty percent of the population were Pushtuns. Meanwhile, to the south of Soviet-occupied Afghanistan are the Baluchi-inhabited areas of Pakistan and Iran. Some 2.5 million of these people live in Pakistan and about a million are on the Iranian side of the border. The existing unrest and the potential for future trouble in the area takes on even graver concern than just the potential for a Soviet-dominated warm water port when one realizes that "greater Baluchistan" includes that part of Iran that controls the Straits of Hormuz, through which all Persian Gulf oil must pass. The Kurds of Iran, Iraq, and Turkey are also a potential target for disruptive and separatist activities, as well as several other other ethnic groups in the tier region.

Obviously the Reagan Administration will be required to develop a policy for how best to deal with such challenges. With the Pakistanis and Turks, military sales and assistance will undoubtedly be high on the list of potential actions. However, in terms of hostile regimes like Khomeini's Iran, the new Administration will face a severe test in terms of how best to prevent Soviet gains.

The war between Iran and Iraq reflects the type of ongoing tensions that can erupt into open hostilities. Iraq was forced to make concessions on the issue of the Shatt-al-Arab, a river that had marked the border between the two countries. In exchange, Iran promised to terminate support for the Kurdish insurgents, who were enjoying periods of considerable success against Iraqi forces.

Thus, at the first opportunity when Iran's previously superior military power seemed to have been sufficiently weakened, the Iraqis struck at Iran, seizing the previously disputed riverine area and continuing into Iran's oil-producing region. Of course, it should be noted that Iraq was also concerned that the Ayatollah Khomeini's Shiite Islamic revolution was beginning to create some problems within the Iraqi Shiite community — which comprises over half of Iraq's population. This situation was particularly sensitive for the government in Baghdad, since it is Sunni-controlled.

It can be expected that the war will continue, possibly with ceasefires, but Iran will bide its time until there is a reasonable probability of regaining its territory. In the meantime, the some three and a half million barrels of oil Iraq was exporting per day will be off the world market, probably for a long time. Furthermore, if Iraq is able to begin exporting oil in the near future, Iran, with little doubt, will be prepared to sink any tankers attempting to carry Iraqi oil out of the Persian Gulf. Likewise, considerable efforts will be made to keep pipelines inoperable if they are located where Iraqi oil could be transported.

On the Arabian peninsula the long-range stability and friendship of the oil-rich, traditional regimes will be of great concern to the Reagan government. Saudi Arabia and the United Arab Emirates are traditionally friendly to the United States and are strongly anti-Communist. Consequently, the new President will have some very cooperative allies when it comes to attempting to reduce Soviet influence in the region.

On the other hand, these governments will also argue that the greatest direct threat they now face emanates from the lack of a peaceful settlement of the Arab-Israeli conflict, including the need for Palestinian self-determination and resolving the question of Jerusalem's status. Such unresolved issues, these anti-Communist leaders will argue, are what provides the Soviets a foothold in the region. These same conservative regimes will be interested in seeing a much more vigorous American policy of protecting their longtime friends, but not basing forces on their soil.

The Reagan response to this complex issue will probably be to emphasize the building of increased American strength and a change of perception about how the United States treats its friends and allies.

In this regard, the new American government will face yet another particularly challenging situation. As a test of the commitment of the new leaders to changing the image of the United States, the oil-rich countries (and/or those generally pro-American states they financially support) will be requesting new American military

weapons. They will likely argue that such equipment is
essential to their defense. Each can easily produce proof
that a potentially belligerent neighbor has equivalent
types of weapons or superior manpower.

The Saudis will undoubtedly establish the case that
they cannot presently adequately defend the oil fields
unless they continue to receive less manpower-intensive
sophisticated weaponry such as the F-15s. Furthermore,
they will probably point to the existence of neighboring
Marxist-ruled South Yemen, which has been involved in
border conflicts with them as well as with North Yemen.
The Saudis might also indicate their concern over the
possibility of attack coming from either Iran or Iraq at
varying points in time. In addition, Riyadh may also
argue that it can best help this country to make the
region safe from communism by purchasing American
weapons for friendly, less resource-fortunate countries
— Somalia, Sudan, Jordan, and others.

Such arguments would place the new Administration
in an extremely difficult situation, since it will need to
encourage a high level of Saudi oil production over the
next several years without simultaneously upsetting
Israeli leaders. The new leaders in Washington may want
to send a message to Moscow and its surrogates that the
"free ride" is over in places like South Yemen and
Ethiopia. Consequently, they should be willing to supply
reasonable types and amounts of weapons and even
train forces to create credible self-defense capabilities
in the conservative countries of the region.

Another Arab country certain to expect considerable
American cooperation in the supply of weapons is Egypt.
President Anwar Sadat will be anxious to demonstrate to
the other Arab states, as well as to the Soviet Union, that
he has the support of the new American government. He
will certainly want a continuation of the modernization
program for his armed forces. Likewise, the Egyptian
leader will want to resume the peace process and dem-

onstrate to President Reagan that he is a man of peace who will continue striving toward that goal.

President Reagan's response, not surprisingly, can be expected to endorse further movement in the peace process, and he will predictably be enthusiastic about providing support for the highly popular (in this country) Anwar Sadat. Indeed, even while observing that conflict and tension are endemic in the Arab world, Mr. Reagan has been quick to point out that specific Arab states such as Egypt may be able and prepared to occupy a front-line position in defending the security of the free world.

To the West, Libya's President Muammar Qaddafi can be expected to support insurgencies throughout the Middle East and elsewhere. Accordingly, he will continue to be a source of great instability and a leader of great concern to President Sadat, whom he has vowed to overthrow. The Soviet presence in Libya is not apt to diminish, and Moscow will almost surely continue to enjoy the advantage of having the use of important military facilities in Libya. The latter are particularly significant because of the large Soviet fleet on station in the Mediterranean.

Recognizing the seriousness of America's military posture in the Middle East region, the Reagan Administration will work diligently to increase the ability of the United States to project force in the area. It can be expected to take advantage of opportunities to utilize military facilities along both the Indian Ocean and Mediterranean littorals in an attempt to be prepared to protect American interests throughout the region and to exploit targets of opportunity that will impact negatively on the Soviet position in the region. However, the Soviets are in a particularly strong position in Yemen, Ethiopia, Afghanistan, Libya, and Iraq. In terms of the Iranian-Iraqi war Moscow has enjoyed a position of overall gain. A Soviet client is winning the war, and Iran's future survival as a large, united entity is becoming more dubious over the long term. Even release of the American hostages would not radically alter the picture.

Thus, the Reagan Administration inherited a Middle Eastern region that is partly on fire and partly ready to explode in its entirety, a domestic economy that is critically dependent upon the petroleum emanating from the region, and an American national interest that requires a peaceful, stable Middle East. The reality is that the new Administration must deal with a region continually on the brink of local and area-wide wars in which instability abounds.

Perhaps nowhere is the combination of hopelessness and hopefulness better exemplified than in the small but miraculous country of Lebanon. Torn apart by its own sixteen different religious sects, used as a battleground by the Israelis and Palestinians, abused sometimes worse than a pawn by the superpowers, finally occupied with the acquiescence of the latter by neighboring Syria, the country still survives. The nation thrives through the spirit of free enterprise and all of the individual initiative that such a system engenders. This exists, despite the ravages of a civil war, largely because sponsored by external actors. Since Lebanon is in many ways a microcosm of the Middle East, it may become a particularly important element of policy for the Reagan Administration.

Small but strategically located, Lebanon could be considered the nerve center of the Middle East. Actions occurring in that country have ramifications throughout the region. Indeed, the present precarious situation radiates far beyond regional concerns; any conflict, particularly in that area, involves the danger of a superpower confrontation.

For the United States, a stable Lebanon would be important for a number of reasons, including what that would contribute toward bringing about and maintaining peace in the Middle East. In the long run, the best way to accomplish the goal of stability would be to work with the moderate Lebanese who are seeking to achieve the democratization of their country. However, as the purpose of this discussion is to look at the needs of, and immediate challenges to, the new Administration, it should be sufficient to note that the long and complicated process of democratization will undoubtedly be supported by the Reagan Administration.

The more urgent problem may well be to begin finding a solution that would enable Lebanon to be returned to the control of Lebanese and prevent foreign powers from occupying the country and using it for a battleground. Here there are several options the new Administration might decide to exercise.

Probably the easiest and least risky avenue would be to increase the quantity and quality of the arms sold to Lebanon and speed up the delivery of those weapons. Another action that could logically follow or even accompany the latter decision would be a strong diplomatic effort to encourage Syria to withdraw from Beirut and allow the Lebanese army to take control of the city. The United States could even become the ultimate guarantor. Of course, this approach could also apply to the eventual withdrawal of the Syrian/Arab League forces from the remainder of the country.

An early, strong American effort could have beneficial effects even beyond specific action. Indeed, the new American leadership may decide that Lebanon is the right place to demonstrate that the United States is serious about regaining its credibility and will take the necessary, well-weighed risks. Stabilizing Lebanon could be a major step down the road toward an ultimate Middle East peace. Certainly a strife-torn, occupied Lebanon under frequent attack is in no one's interest; but in the vacuum of power caused by several years of American inaction events have limped toward disaster.

Just as Lebanon is a microcosm of the region, the Middle East itself represents a microcosm of the third world. Included are resource-poor countries and those rich in resources trying to leap over centuries of development to reach the late twentieth century. In the process, among the newer states, far too many unsettled disputes exist between neighbors and far too many shooting hostilities. Distrust leads to the procurement of vast amounts of weapons, and the Soviet Union is in evidence trying to exploit every unfortunate situation that occurs by attempting to create targets of opportunity, even while the international interest of the United States is best served by stability.

Thus, the scenario for the Reagan Administration is quite clear. Challenges to the United States will continue at a time when this country is, in a relative sense, less strong than it has ever been in the post-World War II era. Yet, more than ever, we require strength to survive in the highly competitive economic, political, and military world in which we live.

Nonetheless, despite the myriad threats to peace and stability around the world facing the new government, it is safe to predict the Reagan response — to regain respect for this country so that friends will be reassured in their trust and potential friends need not fear the consequences of supporting America. Clearly, President Reagan is determined that no group will ever again hold this nation or its people hostage. Because of recent years of neglect, the short-run cost will not be cheap. But in the long run America can afford nothing less.

13

OPPORTUNITIES IN THE WESTERN HEMISPHERE

PEDRO A. SANJUAN

The process of foreign policy formulation is not subject to rigid rules or inflexible formulas. It might be described as the development of a series of initiatives and responses to challenges undertaken in order to guarantee the preservation of national security. When these initiatives are erratic and the responses ineffectual, we say that a foreign policy is lacking. Which does not imply that we have in mind the preparation of a "manual" on foreign policy or that anyone can predict exactly what a successful U.S. foreign policy should be.

Since we cannot control the frequency or determine the nature of the challenges the United States will have to meet during the next four years, to try to predict the exact nature of American foreign policy would be absurd. Even more absurd would be to try to ascertain in advance the specific character a policy toward Latin America, a not necessarily homogeneous part of the world, to which we give an all-inclusive classification for the sake of convenience. What we can attempt to do is delineate sectors of concern.

161

It is appropriate that we begin to give some thought to the need for a change in attitude toward what we call "Latin America" by first realizing that both the United States and Canada are part of that concept; the "North" is not juxtaposed against the "South" in cultural or historical terms, only in terms of geography. Perhaps as many as 50 million persons in the United States today are of "Latin" origin if we count those who speak Spanish, those of French extraction, and those of Italian ancestry. A large part of Canada also enjoys a French tradition. The history, economy, and customs of more than half of what today comprises the United States were linked to the Spanish Empire before passing to the jurisdiction of the United States or directly linked to Mexico before its conquest and annexation. Thus, we too are part of Latin America. In that sense the concept of "Latin America" is meaningful.

But when "Latin America" is used to refer exclusively to the Iberian descendants south of our borders, we come to grips with a less poetic reality: "Latin America" is by no means a homogeneous region, and the United States should address the theme of its relations with this part of the world in terms of bilateral issues with a number of independent and sovereign countries. Nevertheless, we can also recognize the existence of common objectives within a hemispheric relationship, a regional relationship not unlike that we share with Japan or Western Europe. There are pragmatic and compelling, real reasons for hemispheric cooperation based on a new sense of mutual respect and common need.

A new economic relationship is needed to encourage the vigorous development of industry and trade in a hemisphere within which there are various significant poles of burgeoning economic growth. This new economic relationship will not challenge, but should supplement, the traditional industrial and commercial axis occupied by the United States and Canada. The new economic poles are: Argentina in the southern cone; Brazil, well on the way to becoming an industrial giant that will give new meaning to the concept of an Atlantic Community; Venezuela, with its Caribbean orientation; and Mexico, the awakening industrial and energy-producing power of North and Central America. The successful resolution of economic problems in these and the other nations of Latin America is an essential factor in the development of our own and Canada's economic future. In the decade of the eighties this process of growth and development will also play an increasingly important role in the economic viability of the Free World.

The consolidation of political stability and the evolution of lasting institutions in Latin America are as important as growth and the development of a large employment base. Insurance against terrorists and other forces seeking to disrupt through violence the normal evolution of a free market economy cannot be predicated solely on the establishment of a vigorous industrial and commercial base, a process well under way, in the major countries of Latin America.

We share common economic problems with the rest of this Hemisphere — or with the rest of "Latin America." Some common economic problems are:

1. An energy problem common to all the countries in this Hemisphere, for even the oil-rich countries must diversify their energy sources or they will rapidly squander the wealth they now possess in fossil reserves. With the utilization of the most *up-to-date U.S. technology, vast reserves of heavy crude are available in Canada, the United States, and Venezuela.* Concerted policies arrived at in a hemispheric context by the producers of heavy crude, by the refiners, and by the consumers may go a long way toward achieving energy self-sufficiency within the Hemisphere.

2. The other industrialized countries of this Hemisphere are fully committed to the development of advanced nuclear fuel technology and a broader nuclear energy base to complement their present reliance on conventional energy sources. If the United States does not work together with the rest of the Hemisphere toward this common goal, safeguarded by hemispheric agreements eschewing the development and use of nuclear weapons by common consent and purpose, *the Soviet Union will eventually become the principal purveyor of such technology, backed by Soviet concessional financing.* Much to everybody's detriment in this Hemisphere, Soviet commercial competition in the nuclear or in any other field would eventually undermine the security of the entire Hemisphere.

3. Traditionally, the orientation of Latin America has been toward the development of overseas markets for its raw materials. Its customers have been Europe and the United States. *As industrialization progresses, the Hemisphere must encourage competitive development of markets across national borders,* not for the still unsellable raw material exports of the recent past, but for the increasing volume of today's and tomorrow's consumer goods, refined fuel and derivative products, and diversified agricultural exports. The United States should take part in this process as a full partner and not as a principal exporter of finished industrial products and primary importer of raw materials. Hemispheric interdependence in trade is a relationship that will benefit the United States as well as its neighbors. Immigration and emigration are part of the economic syndrome.

4. Countries like Mexico — the sources of much of the cheap labor available in certain parts of the United States — are themselves the intermediate or ultimate

destination of immigrants from other countries in this Hemisphere. The *immigration problems should be addressed intelligently, gradually, and in the spirit of interdependence that will ensure the ultimate benefit of all the nations involved and protect the human rights of the individuals concerned.*

Defense of the Hemisphere is a very real concern. The Sovietization of this Hemisphere is against the interest of all those whose rising aspirations envisage participation in the broadening of the economic benefits of a free enterprise system geared to a rising consumer market. Soviet socialism inhibits wealth distribution because it inhibits the creation of wealth. It "eliminates" unemployment by sanctioning massive underproductivity, creates economic and social "equality" by reducing everyone to an unacceptable level of poverty, and imposes an ideological compliance that leads to the worst kind of spiritual poverty.

From the general we may now go into the more specific opportunities. Cuba is the best example. Although Castro has been failing miserably inside Cuba in social, political, and economic terms, U.S. actions have been so confused and easily manipulated by the theatrical Cuban leader that they have actually contributed to increasing Castro's international stature.

Fidel Castro is not ten feet tall. Actually, he's a dismal failure. Almost a million of his most productive fellow Cubans have left the island and found a home in Florida. Through their intelligence and industry within the system of free enterprise Castro destroyed in Cuba, they have become one of the most thriving communities in the United States.

Castro has no system to export to anybody. He is not a world leader, or a worthy antagonist of the United

States, or a revolutionary hero in Cuba. He is a man capable only in the art of maintaining personal power in a country he oppresses, in an economy he has caused to deteriorate rather than improve, in a once-proud nation he has reduced to the status of a servile puppet of the Soviet Union.

For just over two decades we have dealt with Fidel Castro through a form of "respectful" antagonism. We have unwittingly provided him with stature in the third world. We have created a myth about his ability to withstand the wrath of the U.S. colossus. The image of Castro, which we are doing little or nothing to puncture, is that in spite of the U.S. embargo, he has been capable of thriving economically.

This myth is very far from the chronic reality of Castro's Cuba. For today, *more than twenty years after the revolution,* stringent rationing still exists in Cuba, rationing so rigorous that large numbers of people in Havana are going hungry in a so-called "egalitarian" society.

The present Cuban system of education has done little to increase literacy. Cuba had one of the Hemisphere's highest literacy rates before the revolution. It was 77 percent in 1953, six years before Castro took power. Since then his educational reform has resulted in the complete destruction of the previous system of free education. Today many students are forced into careers in which they have no interest.

The notion of "no unemployment" is a fiction of Castro's deceptive propaganda, albeit one we seldom challenge. In fact, Cuba has enormous unemployment problems. This is principally evident in Castro's ability and willingness to export Cuban cannon fodder to Africa and other parts of the world. In a country where the economy is underproductive, excess labor, particularly from among the youth, is conscripted and sent to fight in foreign lands. Young Cuban soldiers frequently return in pine boxes. Thus, the "system" encompasses both a short-term and a more permanent solution to the Cuban unemployment problem. Another Cuban way of solving the embarrassing evidence of unemployment is to assign the same task to several people so that everyone "looks" employed.

The Cuban socialist economy began with the total destruction of the Cuban free enterprise system. Cuba's economy was a shambles during and after the revolution. It continued a shambles during the period of revolutionary consolidation. And it remains a shambles today, twenty long years after the revolution promised to provide equality and abundance for everyone in a people's paradise.

A burdensome Soviet subsidy barely bails out Fidel's bankrupt economy. Cuba, which trades with most of the world today, has been essentially insolvent each year of the twenty years since the revolution. Today Cuban advisers in Nicaragua, special envoys of Fidel Castro, occasionally advise their Nicaraguan fellow revolutionaries not to destroy the private sector as Fidel did two decades ago. That, they point out, has been economic suicide in Cuba.

According to World Bank statistics, Cuba's average per capita Gross National Product from 1960 to 1977, the last available year, has actually *declined* by 0.2 percent per year. Castro's Cuba is one of the few countries in the world that has shown such a consistent economic decline over so many years. In 1959 Cuba had the third largest per capita income in the Hemisphere. Today it ranks eleventh, having been surpassed by many countries that have not seen the need to enslave their people in order to promote a program of development. Twentieth-century socialism has proved to be an economic system subordinated to a series of political objectives that guarantee the continued distribution of scarcity, even poverty. But Fidel Castro has gone beyond that point. He is an incompetent socialist, even when measured against socialism's usual failures.

Instead of coherent policies, Fidel Castro has instituted his own personal whim. The most inane and insane purpose of Castro's flamboyant, but actually tragic, rule of Cuba has been his war on the city of Havana. At an earlier time Havana was one of the most beautiful and vital urban areas of this Hemisphere. Castro's concept of the revolution's prime objective was to raise the level of the countryside and punish the "evil" of Havana. The countryside has experienced the minimal benefits of some showcase hospitals, schools, and day care centers. But the Cuban farmer still lives in inadequate housing, characterized by the single light bulb, the dirt floor, and no plumbing. Castro's rural reforms show small progress after twenty years of socialist activity. Castro's urban objective to strangle Havana deliberately and slowly has reduced that once lovely city to something resembling an enormous slum. What could such an objective accomplish? Cuban socialism provides no model for the other nations of the Caribbean.

Instead of working to create better conditions for economic development in Cuba, Castro concentrates his efforts on exporting revolution to the Caribbean and Central America. Instead of diversifying his one-crop economy, he concentrates his efforts on spreading the doctrine of violence and terror as legitimate forms of political expression in order to undermine the process of social and economic evolution in Central America or in little destitute islands like Granada.

The result is inevitably and monotonously predictable. The shaky economies he undermines will be set back ten to twenty years. Poverty and scarcity will become generalized. Paralysis and isolation will become the trademarks of the new regimes that follow the example set in Cuba more than twenty years ago. Countries with a history of sectoral poverty will become economies of general disaster. This is the new socialist order. Equality means "nothing for everybody."

This paradise of privation and hunger has to be paid for with personal sacrifices. Political liberty is abolished; food rationing is instituted and institutionalized; and opposition is eliminated by the use of summary justice and the expansion of the criminal code to encompass broad new categories of political crimes.

Signs derisively critical of Castro have begun to appear throughout Havana, in public places and in cemeteries. Robberies and other forms of lawlessness have increased dramatically.

In January and February of this year Fidel decided to act. All cabinet ministers were fired. Fidel Castro himself took charge of the Ministry of Internal Affairs (Gobernacion), of Defense, and of Economic Development. New repressive measures were instituted as the popular challenge to Fidel increased. But the new terror appeared to be of no avail.

Cuba is an unfortunate reality of today. It represents as well a harrowing possibility — a possibility of which the United States must be continually aware.

In the Caribbean there exists a significant political polarity between the two largest islands, Cuba and Puerto Rico. The failure of Cuban *state socialism,* loosely patterned after the Soviet system, or of Puerto Rican *free enterprise capitalism,* loosely patterned after the U.S. system — or even the semblance of temporary failure in either case — will have important repercussions in the rest of the Caribbean.

It is true that this perception has been put forth frequently during the last three decades, so frequently as to make it seem almost less urgent today than the most common truism.

At the height of the euphoria that was prevalent during the Alliance for Progress the likelihood that conditions would develop to justify an invidious comparison at the expense of Puerto Rican free enterprise appeared remote. Yet today there is real danger of the long-range collapse of Puerto Rico's economic viability and subsequently of its political stability.

The economy of Puerto Rico is going through a critical period of transition, a transition from the formulas that worked well in the past, but are failing today, to the still unresolved solutions of the future. The success of the economic plans implemented by Muñoz and his lieutenants in the last three decades brought forth the rise in the island's living standard. A higher living standard in turn raised minimum wage level demands. Yet, without an available supply of cheap skilled labor — and in spite of the continuation of liberal tax exemption benefits recently instituted by the present government of Puerto Rico — continental U.S. and foreign manufacturers tend to regard Puerto Rico as no longer an investor's paradise. Tourism has also ebbed, in spite of seasonal upsurges resulting from the cold winters recently experienced in the continental United States. Actual unemployment on the island has been estimated recently to be as high as 20 percent or higher. Two-thirds of the population depend on food stamps. Labor unrest continues to grow.

The domestic concerns of the United States and the priorities of U.S. foreign policy have caused our attention to vault over the Caribbean for the last two decades, if we exclude our objection to Cuba's role in Africa or the construction of nuclear submarine pens and the presence of high performance Soviet aircraft in Cuba. At present we should be anticipating with considerable alarm the political and economic crisis engulfing most of the area. We should be meeting this crisis with meaningful attempts at reversing the downward economic spiral and the threat to the possible dissolution of what up to now have been democratic societies.

Our Latin American policy has fluctuated between benign neglect and certain manifestations of what we prefer to regard as a confrontation among friends. The Panama Canal treaties have consumed our domestic political energies (pro or con), and many Americans have accepted the ratification of these treaties as a great milestone in our relations with all of Latin America, including the Caribbean. Thus the intensity of attention required by the pressing problems of the Caribbean has been so far conspicuously absent in the U.S. Some of the most urgent concerns are:

1. The economic and political viability of federations that were former British colonies — St. Kitts-Nevis-Anguilla.

2. Sources of economic development funds for the Caribbean area, which has little institutional political clout among the boards of directors of international lending institutions.

3. Opportunities for varied small-scale investments in basic labor-intensive industries throughout the Caribbean — correlation with markets in the U.S., Canada, and Europe.

4. The "multifaceted" solution to the economic resurgence of Puerto Rico, a sophisticated formula that could be applied either under statehood or the revised commonwealth status.

5. U.S. corporate concerns in the Caribbean and the extent of the present political threat to U.S. business interests.

6. Essential factors affecting U.S. national security in the Caribbean.

Of the utmost urgency and greatest significance to the felicitous future development of the Caribbean is Edward Seaga's recent victory in Jamaica. In spite of his stunning victory, Seaga inherits a ruined economy, thanks to the socialist experiments of his predecessor. Neither the economic assistance programs the Carter Administration had planned before the outcome of the Jamaican election, which provided meager economic support and marginal PL 480 funds, nor the upward revision presented to Congress in November 1980 will be adequate to help Seaga return his country to a solvent status.

On November 7 President-elect Reagan said at a news conference: "With regard to the countries of South America, Central America, and here on the North American continent our two neighbors, I've repeatedly made it plain that I think over the years we have let relationships deteriorate. And this should not be. And we are going to make every effort to bring together, by way of bilateral agreements and so forth, the peoples of the Americas so that North and Central and South America can be united in their determination to be free."

Perhaps nowhere is the need to avoid deterioration greater than in Mexico. Yet in seeking to do so we should recognize that the Mexican political reality is very different from ours, very complex, and sometimes seemingly inscrutable. Nevertheless, considerable attention was paid by the media during the Presidential campaign to the signs of reaction in Mexico, both popular and official, to a Reagan victory. Perhaps because Mexico's political atmosphere is so different from ours, we in the United States have had a tendency to misread these signs.

To accept such generalities in the American press as "Mexico is hoping for a Carter victory" was difficult, even when they came from persons presumably on the scene. Officially, there were no comments on the U.S. Presidential campaign from the government of Mexico. Indeed, President Lopez Portillo's statement when he was in Brazil that it makes no difference who sits in the Oval Office seemed to indicate there was a correct Mexican policy of not intervening in the domestic politics of the United States, a country with large numbers of voters of Mexican origin. Certainly the President of Mexico and his administration understood that just as Mexicans jealously and proudly guard their internal political process from foreign interference, we in the United States would react adversely to foreign efforts to influence our choice of President.

In discussions with influential Mexicans the impression one gets is *not* of Mexican opposition to the Reagan Administration, but rather of Mexican interest and curiosity. In many cases this interest has been accentuated by a keen appreciation of past U.S. ineptness, as in the abrupt cancellation of the natural gas agreements with Mexico.

Essentially, the serious problems between Mexico and the United States during the last four years have stemmed from a lack of respect for the importance of Mexico as a sovereign collaborator in the process of solving many problems we both share and in establishing a durable symbiotic relationship.

The strategic importance of a stable and secure Western Hemisphere to the national security interests of the United States should be evident. A hemisphere fragmented, at war with itself, will be of unusual detriment to economic development and to United States interests as well.

From the Cuban missile crisis, which brought the world close to World War III, to the El Salvador-Honduras border war and, more recently, border altercations between Nicaragua and Costa Rica, the Organization of American States has functioned as the regional instrument called in to deal with sudden crisis. As a working system it is a more effective instrument for dealing with hemispheric conflicts than the more unwieldly United Nations system and has kept many regional problems from spilling over onto the world stage. Further weakening of the OAS can result in the United Nations assuming jurisdiction in Latin American regional problems, with the prospect of a Soviet veto, as well as in bringing the panorama of East-West issues into the debate on Western Hemisphere problems.

The United States has traditionally seen the OAS as useful in promoting political and security objectives in the Hemisphere. Although supporting collective security ideals, most Latin Americans have regarded the OAS chiefly as a means to restrain U.S. power and as a forum to present united Latin American views to the United States. This difference, in perspective, takes the form of U.S. interest in the OAS as a mechanism to promote individual and political rights, reduce tensions among states within the region, and possibly to foster regional arms constraint — compared with the predominant Latin American view that accepts the utility of such activity, but is most concerned with the OAS as a forum to promote economic development. OAS bodies such as the Pan American Health Organization have contributed importantly to the quality of life in the Americas.

The mutual defense treaty of the Western Hemisphere, better known as the Rio Treaty, antedates the North Atlantic Treaty Organization. In its application through the OAS over the years, this treaty has served the Hemisphere well in dealing with aggression and threats or fears of aggression, as well as in calming disputes that might have led to actual conflict. Not surprisingly, at the Non-Aligned Conference last year in Havana, Castro attempted unsuccessfully to dismantle the Rio Treaty.

In terms of the rest of this Hemisphere, despite close historic, geographic, and treaty relations, the United States, in recent years, has sent contradictory and confusing signals. As a consequence, there is a growing belief that Washington's interest in the regional forum of the OAS — apart from its political attributes — is marginal. Unfortunately, the announced intention to reduce funding for the OAS, including the voluntary funds designated for technical assistance, has been interpreted by representatives of other governments as loss of United States interest in the entire regional system. Conclusions were drawn among member states that the planned budgetary reductions themselves were based upon political, not financial, considerations.

Multilateral forums such as the OAS are at best imperfect and at worst inefficient. Multilateral diplomacy cannot be a substitute for traditional bilateral relationships, but it can be a most important supplement and complement. The United States can work more easily with individual governments on concrete problems than with groups of governments on abstract principles. Yet time and again United States interests are also better served by working with allies legally protecting their position, as was the example in the Cuban missile crisis. It was the vote of the OAS that gave legal basis for the quarantine against Cuba, and our allies' willingness to follow the leadership of the United States was a heavy and unexpected blow to the Soviets.

It is imperative to search for an effective mode of cooperation whenever possible in order to avoid confrontation. The OAS is an appropriate and effective forum for the most powerful state in the world and the rest of the American States to meet freely, in order to discuss, determine, smooth out, and possibly attenuate the differences that at times separate us.

In United States relations within this Hemisphere there has been a kind of boom-and-bust cycle, an ebb-and-flow, peak-and-valley syndrome of United States interest. When the United States awakens to a perceived threat to its interests, it launches a grand new hemispheric initiative — a Good Neighbor Policy, an Alliance for Progress, a New Dialogue. Hopes are aroused and pressures mount for the United States to fulfill its promises. When the overly optimistic expectations are deflated, the U.S. is quickly charged with infidelity. Time after time the cycle repeats itself.

Events in the Caribbean and Central America in particular have shown that many of these economic problems are global in nature and require global approaches for their solution. Yet a global solution through the world forum of the United Nations is much too gradual an approach to the explosion resulting from unresolved problems.

The recent United States tendency has been to look at the Hemisphere outside the terms of a special relationship. This approach tends to challenge the very conceptual basis of a separate regional organization. Such lack of a clearly defined role for the OAS, beyond peacekeeping and human rights, suggests that serious rethinking is urgent if the OAS and the Inter-American system as presently consituted are to survive.

The United States has not always had the support within the OAS for everything it has done. Frequently United States patience has been sorely tried by opposition of some of the larger countries to measures the United States felt to be in the common interest and worthy of support. Historically, however, on issues of great importance to the United States the other countries of this Hemisphere have supported the United States.

An implicit assumption is that the United States will not abandon the OAS as a regional organization in favor of a smaller association bound together by military ties or by some other limited common denominator but progressively deprived of its character and authority as a regional organization.

The foregoing has been a general survey of some of the less publicized opportunities that are readily available for fast improvement of relations between the United States and the other nations of this Hemisphere, including Cuba, if we recognize that "Cuba" as a concept embodies the ultimate fulfillment of the will of a people and not the continued imposition of the will of a totalitarian government.

14

OF MICE AND PAPER TIGERS: EUROPE IN DISARRAY

H. JOACHIM MAITRE

Shame on you Athenians for not wishing to understand that in war one must not allow oneself to be at the command of events. You Athenians are the strongest of all the Greeks in ships, infantry, cavalry, and revenue. But you do not make the best of them. You make war like a barbarian when he wrestles: If he suffers a blow, he immediately puts his hand to it. If he is struck again, he puts his hand there. But he has not the skill to evade his antagonist, nor does he think of parrying the blow. You likewise, if you hear that Philip has attacked the Chaeronea, you send help there. If he is at Thermopylae, you run there. If he turns aside, you follow him to right or left as if you were acting on his orders. Never a fixed plan, never any precautions. You wait for bad news before you act.

Demosthenes
(circa 351 B.C.)
in *First Philippic*

After Reagan's landslide victory, Western European statesmen commented in unison, "A resolute America is a relief to us." An exception was Gaston Thorn, Luxembourg's foreign minister and current president of the European Common Market Council of Ministers, who openly voiced his fear that the U.S. might now turn isolationist: "There has been a move to the right, and there is reason to fear that the United States will turn inward. This could have harsh consequences for Europe." President Reagan must steer U.S. foreign policy in that vast ocean separating a "resolute" America from an isolationist one. He inherits European alliances in disarray at a time when the Atlantic relationships assume greater importance. Difficult problems of European coordination face President Reagan in an era of energy and mineral scarcity, developing countries' antagonism, and detente's demise.

Despite four years of President Carter's diluted defense budgets and bleak economic record, the nations of Europe still regard the United States of America as "the strongest in ships, infantry, cavalry, and revenue." However, Europeans also believe that Americans do not make the best of these assets, that they still seem to be convinced there are no problems with NATO's only superpower that better management will not cure. But they are not fully aware of the huge number of U.S. Navy ships recently stored in mothballs, the Strategic Air Command's emaciated bomb wings, the teething troubles of the Army's new main battle tank (XM-1), and the Marine Corps' F/A 18 and AV-8 attack aircraft, or the impact of low wages and inflation on retention rates in all services of the U.S. Armed Forces.

If the Carter Presidency's national security and foreign policy — or lack of it: "Never a fixed plan, never any precautions" — has suffered blow after blow, in Nicaragua, in Iran, in the United nations, in Afghanistan, the new man in the White House is always thought capable of repairing the greater part of the damage. In this spirit, Britain's *Daily Telegraph* congratulated President-elect Ronald Reagan "on his appointment as sheriff of the free world's most important county."

Unfortunately, such magnanimous confidence in America's inviolable might often camouflages the glaring shortcomings in Western Europe's own contribution to the West's collective security. During the 1980s this shortcoming will prove more apparent and dangerous. Europeans, however, have felt reassured by Ronald Reagan's campaign speeches as Presidential candidate, in particular by his words on foreign policy in the final TV debate with President Carter: "The burden of maintaining the peace falls on us. To maintain that peace requires strength. America has never gotten into a war because we were too strong. We can get into a war by letting events get out of hand . . . We must have a consistent foreign policy, a strong America . . . and then build up our national security, to restore our margin of safety, and at the same time try to restrain the Soviet buildup."

Western Europeans face the evidence of the Soviet arms buildup — particularly its acceleration in the late 1970s — and have been pretending so far that the move merely reflects Russia's traditional fear of foreign aggression and is "defensive in nature." In the Federal Republic of Germany this ludicrous view has been propagated by, among others, Herbert Wehner, a former Communist and now the Social Democrats' party whip in the Bundestag, by Theo Sommer, editor in chief of the influential liberal weekly *Die Zeit* (Hamburg), and by Bundeswehr General Gert Bastian, until recently commanding the 12th Armored Division. Chancellor Helmut Schmidt, who explicitly does not share this pipe-dream interpretation of Soviet intentions, has nevertheless contributed to its effect by proposing a "temporary halt" in the deployment of new American nuclear missiles in Western Europe.

The Soviet arms buildup is massive and well documented. In 1979 alone the Soviet Union produced 3,000 main battle tanks, 1,800 combat aircraft, 4,000 armored troop carriers, and 250 new intercontinental missiles. During the last decade the Soviet armed forces introduced four new types of intercontinental missiles, a new breed of tank, a new family of tactical aircraft and the world's largest fleet of attack helicopters. The result, many American and European analysts agree, is that (1) the USSR is close to achieving breakthrough superiority in Central Europe; (2) NATO would have to use nuclear weapons to stop such an assault; (3) the Soviets have built up a lead in tactical nuclear weapons also, thus limiting Western options while expanding their fleet of transport aircraft and surface ships so that they can land their troops more quickly anywhere in Asia and Africa than can the West; and (4) the USSR also punctured the American "nuclear umbrella" by achieving at least parity in long-range nuclear delivery systems.

In contrast, a series of President Carter's unilateral decisions gravely affected Europe's security. He canceled the B-1 strategic bomber and slowed down all other strategic programs: the MX missile, the Trident submarine, the various cruise missiles. He imposed a 5.5 percent ceiling on the salary increases that were supposed to improve the quality of the American All-Volunteer armed forces. President Carter vetoed the Navy's new nuclear carrier *Vinson* and stopped production of the "enhanced radiation warhead" after having arm-twisted German Chancellor Schmidt into asking for this neutron bomb. Production of this revolutionary tank-breaking weapon would be of vital importance to a Western Europe now facing the Warsaw Pact's overwhelming tank thrust. Furthermore, Carter bungled SALT II and in October 1980 entered into European "disarmament" talks with the Soviet Union, jeopardizing deployment of the new "Euromissiles" in Western Europe.

President Carter thus presented NATO with a gamut of reasons for wanting a new man in the White House.

Now that Jimmy Carter is out and Ronald Reagan is in, pledging a revival of NATO ("We believe in the importance of NATO, and we will do everything we can do to reassure our friends that we are not going it alone"), European hopes are also pregnant with misgivings. What about the European side of the NATO coin? Which plans and demands would the new President have in store for NATO's European allies? Immediately after the November elections the *Daily Telegraph* warned: "The correction of the military balance will take several years of determined efforts and resistance to Russia's huffing and puffing. During this time, unless some of America's European allies adjust to the Reagan Presidency and take advantage of the opportunity it offers, disastrous trans-Atlantic tensions could occur."

No prophetic talent is required to predict that President Reagan's stress on defense spending and his apparent no-nonsense approach to Soviet expansionism are bound to foster friction within the Atlantic Alliance. With the exception of the Thatcher government in Britain and that of Prime Minister Sa Carneiro in Portugal, most European governments prefer a range of soft measures that balance their national security against the temptations of detente with the Eastern bloc. The contrast between probable American defense-spending plans and the increasing unwillingness of several European NATO members to comply with existing defense obligations signals the reefs of serious trans-Atlantic disputes. Since the NATO treaty was signed in 1949 several member countries have grown accustomed to riding the back seat, using the Alliance as a convenient framework for listlessness and docility. On the American side tension is also likely to be fueled by the long-standing exasperation of the political Right with Europe's failure to pull its weight in NATO. This irritation will be exacerbated by the recent resurgence of a neutralist trend in the British Labour Party, which after returning to power has already declared its intention of dismantling Britain's nuclear arsenals and banishing American nuclear forces from British soil.

The United States is at odds with several of its European allies over their failure to meet agreed NATO standards calling for an annual 3 percent "real increase" in defense spending. In addition, economically depressed Great Britain claims to be unable to fulfill its commitment and has begun to curtail military procurement and deployment and participation in NATO exercises. West Germany has also announced its plans to cut back to roughly 2 percent. And despite sometimes heavy-handed pressure from Washington, three other allies (Denmark, Belgium, and the Netherlands) — much smaller but by no means poorer — are certain to fall far short of the obligatory 3 percent increase in 1981. Analyzing this ominous trend ("Does NATO Exist?" *The Washington Quarterly,* Fall 1979), Irving Kristol concluded: "The nations of Western Europe seem to have opted out of the strenuous game of world politics in order to pursue the comforts of domestic life."

This trend has gone far. In mid-September Belgium's former foreign secretary, Henri Simonet, publicly accused his country of becoming "the scrounger on NATO" and spoke of the spread of "a rampant neutralism" that would eventually "empty Belgium's contribution to NATO of all substance." Simonet, a member of Belgium's Socialist party, declared: "Participation in Atlantic solidarity is a collaborative effort, and it is without purpose or meaning if limited to the ritual expression of a conviction that no longer bears any relation to the policy actually pursued."

Simonet's bitter outburst was prompted by the indecision of the Belgian government about the stationing of new American missiles in Belgium, in accordance with the December 1979 NATO agreement. The agreement called for deployments by 1982-83 of 464 cruise missiles (GLCM) and 108 medium-range "Pershing 2" missiles. Belgium had accepted "in principle" 48 of the GLCMs, the rest being distributed to Holland (48), Britain (160), Italy (112), and Germany (96). Germany had accepted all of the 108 Pershing 2s, to be operated there by U.S. troops. But the Dutch soon announced that a "final decision" would have to wait until the end of 1981, arguing that they wished to await probable progress in negotiations between the U.S.A. and the U.S.S.R. on limiting the growth of the "theater nuclear" arsenal in Europe. Belgium soon followed the Dutch example.

The importance of the deployment of these U.S. missiles rests in the fact that the whole of Western Europe lies within easy reach of the Soviet triple-warhead SS-20 medium-range mobile missiles already deployed in the Soviet Union. Both the new American GLCMs and the Pershing 2s are needed urgently to counter the ever growing threat from the SS-20s. The Belgian move to block deployment confirms the worst fears of those Europeans and Americans who see Belgium — once a solid pillar of NATO — slipping steadily into the quasi-neutralist position of the Dutch and the Danes.

A new word exists for this tendency: "Denmarkization." "Denmarkization" occurs when a country decides there is no need to spend much money on its defense, since its allies will be forced to defend it anyway. "Denmarkization" differs from "Finlandization" in that no official declaration of neutrality is required. Although membership in the Alliance continues, contributions dwindle. For example, Denmark spends only 2.2 percent of its GNP on defense (the U.S.A., 5.5 percent), less than any other European NATO members (except Luxembourg, which possesses neither a navy nor an air force). In the autumn of 1980 Denmark's Social Democrat government announced a freeze in its defense budget for the next four years "in real terms." Given the skyrocketing increase in defense equipment, "real terms" means that the Danish defense budget is being cut by 4 percent a year. When measured against the defense commitment accepted by all Danish parties in 1973, these cuts mean that Denmark will have at target date 1985 (1) 30 ships against the 52 projected in 1973, (2) 80 advanced combat aircraft, mostly F-16s, against the original 120, and (3) 120 tanks against 200.

"Denmarkization" has also affected Belgium, which participated only negligibly in the 1980 NATO autumn exercises "on account of rising fuel costs." For the same reason, Belgium's tactical air force, with its 150 aircraft, mostly outdated, has virtually remained grounded in 1980. Belgium's ground forces, numbering roughly 62,000, possess a total of only 175 artillery pieces, but need at least 1,100. Belgium's First Army Corps, entrusted by NATO with the protection of the Northern Army Group's southern flank in Lower Saxony, operates a total of 330 tanks — where 700 are needed. Belgium is no longer a dependable, functioning part of NATO.

In addition to NATO's perennial problems, Norway's refusal to allow nuclear arms on its soil, the eternal squabbling between Turks and Greeks, the enigma of France and its suspended membership, President Reagan will face both an Atlantic Alliance and a Europe in disarray. The illusions of detente have taken their toll, but European trade with the common adversary continues as if Afghanistan had not been invaded. The ambiguous response of European NATO members to that invasion and their failure to understand that the turmoil in the Persian Gulf represents a lethal threat to the freedom and well-being of the vulnerable industrial democracies betray a lack of common purpose as well as a narrowness of purpose.

In 1979 Henry Kissinger declared in Brussels that

"NATO is reaching a point where the strategic assumptions on which it has been operating, the force structures that it has been generating, and the joint policies it has been developing will be inadequate for the 1980s."

When NATO was founded, the U.S. had an overwhelming strategic nuclear superiority. At the time of the Middle East crisis in 1973 — when NATO's European membership, with the laudable exception of Portugal, denied U.S. cargo aircraft en route to Israel permission to refuel or land on their soil — the U.S. enjoyed a strategic superiority of approximately eight to one in missile warheads. Since that time, however, the U.S.S.R. has dramatically increased its number of warheads. If, indeed, it had been the "secret dream of every European that — if there had to be a nuclear war — to have it conducted over their heads by the strategic forces of the United States and the Soviet Union" (Henry Kissinger, "The Future of NATO," *The Washington Quarterly,* Fall 1979), that "dream" has turned to dust as the Soviet Union stands poised to achieve superiority in both strategic and theater nuclear forces. The dire and compelling question as Kissinger stated remains: "How is it possible to survive with these imbalances in the face of the already demonstrated inferiority in conventional forces?"

Western Europe unofficially claims to have found the answer in a European version of detente that "treats detente not as a balancing of national interests and negotiations on the basis of strategic realities but rather as an exercise in strenuous goodwill" (Kissinger). Even after Afghanistan, German Chancellor Schmidt continues to assert that "there will be no shooting as long as the talking goes on." This "dialectic" is composed almost exclusively of the conventional ingredients of diplomacy: national defense, international trade, international discourse. Such a conventional approach is no

longer appropriate in a transformed economic environment. Kissinger considers it "a rash Western policy that
did not take into account that in the decade ahead we
will face simultaneously an unfavorable balance of
power, a world in turmoil, a potential economic crisis,
and a massive energy problem. To conduct business as
usual is to entrust one's destiny to the will of others."

The debate escalates, however. *The Economist* recently hit the crux of NATO's problem, its lethargy, and also
criticized NATO's taboo subject, the international role of
Germany. "The eventual test of West Germany's recovery from the disaster of Hitler would be its return to
the politics of the wider world outside Europe. The Germans now have a chance to recognize that they can help
to meet the challenge to Western interests outside
Europe." This opportunity arises because of the potential German contribution to a balance of military power
against Russia in Southwest Asia.

The Economist concludes that European allies run
great risk in leaving the defense of the Gulf region
almost entirely to America. Secretary of Defense Brown
has said that the United States expects to spend about
$5 billion a year on defending the Gulf. No European
countries, however, have projected any such extra expenditures, in spite of Europe's even greater reliance on
Gulf oil.

"The European members of NATO," says *The Economist*, "who have already been told by America that
they will have to do more to defend Europe itself, may
wake up in a few years' time to find that America's ability to protect Europe. . . would then be entrusting a vital
interest to a handful of American warships and (a presently inadequate) American 'rapid deployment force'. . . .
It is doubtful whether the alliance could sustain such a
one-sided arrangement for many years." Most analysts
doubt such an unbalanced alliance could long endure.

To avoid this untenable situation, Mr. Reagan could

encourage some European NATO countries to lend a hand in Southwest Asia. NATO as such, *The Economist* points out, will probably not do so "because any attempt to do so would probably run into a Danish or a Dutch veto. But individual NATO countries can help. Britain, with a sizable navy, a staging base at Akrotiri in Cyprus, and a political foothold in Oman, can make a contribution. But Britain, with 4.9 percent of its GNP going to defense, is already near the end of its spending tether. Money for the Gulf would have to come out of its forces in Europe, which are already stretched much too thin."

In contrast, Germany's defense spending is only a modest 3.3 percent of a much bigger GNP. Although Germany cannot spend much more on its 335,000-man army, which is about as large as other European countries wish to tolerate, it can, however, usefully expand its navy. Last July West Germany asked for, and got an end to, the World War II restrictions on naval size.

Quoting again from *The Economist*: "This new freedom opens the door to a bigger German navy, which would draw none of the dark glances from other Europeans that a bigger army or air force would."

There is a worse way and a better way for the Germans to use their new freedom of the seas. The worse way would be to build the wrong sort of warships — smallish frigates designed mainly for antisubmarine work in the Atlantic or as antiaircraft missile platforms in the Baltic, giving NATO little extra security in either place. President Reagan should encourage Germany to adopt a better way — that of building at least a few warships useful in the Indian Ocean.

The Economist emphasizes that naval power independent of large land bases "is the West's immediate need in Southwest Asia. This means larger, longer-range ships carrying helicopters, jump-jets, and detachments of naval infantry; warships that can project their power ashore, but spend most of their time at a discreet distance from land."

President Reagan could use the American Tarawa class of amphibious assault ships or the British Invincible class of small aircraft carriers as models. Mr. Reagan can encourage the Germans to look east of Suez, since they can no longer argue either that there is nothing for them to spend more defense money on or that their security interests lie wholly within Europe. There is a tacit agreement that a central purpose of American foreign policy should be to engage the other members of NATO (and Japan, of course) in a common protection of oil and vital raw materials. NATO's semi-member, France, already does its part in Zaire and Chad in the Central African Republic and off the Persian coast. Common European wisdom holds that for the allies to enjoy U.S. protection, without sharing equitably the military and financial responsibilities, can only fuel resentment in America and foster neutralist illusions in Europe.

The stumbling block lies within Germany. No respectable newspaper or journal in West Germany could venture to support *The Economist's* conclusions. No major political party would advocate it and any such action would provoke internal outcries of "militarism!" "adventurism!" and "revanchism!" Now, thirty-five years after World War II, despite the "economic miracle" and full membership in international organizations, despite their alleged leading role in the European Community, the Germans have not left the shadow of the Third Reich's adventurism and barbarism. West Germany is reluctant to become a power again. If military power is a major instrument of foreign policy, West Germany is incapable of playing its part and unwilling to be drawn into a new global role. West Germany is the West's and NATO's paper tiger. It will be Reagan's major challenge in Europe — and the black hole in his foreign policy design.

In his assessment of major problem areas in foreign policy, presented in June 1977 to the Foreign Policy Association in New York City (*United States Foreign Policy and World Realities,* Hoover Institution, Stanford University Press) Ronald Reagan commented on

- *Soviet Expansionism/American Idealism:* "The Soviet Union has a global objective. That fact alone makes our idealism vulnerable. We Americans would dearly love to let everyone live in peace and harmony. This may be described as a global objective, but it is no substitute for coherent global policy in the face of real challenges."

- *Soviet Arms Buildup:* "Despite its huge arms buildup in the past few years, the Soviet Union does not want to fight a war if it can be avoided. Instead, the Soviet buildup seems to be designed primarily for political leverage — to achieve their aims indirectly. . . they want to accomplish the gradual encirclement of the West and reduction of its strategic and economic influence."

- *Detente:* "Detente between the United States and the Soviet Union may actually have improved the climate for Soviet promotion of proxy wars . . . We saw detente as a relaxation of tensions. . . they saw it otherwise. Detente, to the Soviet Union, became a victory for the U.S.S.R. and a growing sign of Western weakness."

- *The West and the World:* "Perhaps the most important reality facing us today is the shrinking global influence of the West. Throughout the West it seems to have engendered in the Western public at large that sense of fatalistic indifference which living by the side of a volcano induces in the population. That difference presents the Western world with its greatest challenge in ages. I am talking not only of Western loss of natural resources and materials, though that is occurring, but beyond it to the decline of the Western concepts of political responsibility and individual freedom."

Many Europeans have expressed concern that Reagan's foreign policy views are bound to compel priorities alien to European objectives. These fears were spelled out prior to the elections. For example, the Social Democrats' Peter Corterier, foreign affairs expert in the Bundestag in Bonn, said: "Detente is the political foundation of NATO. Reagan touches the very nerve of the Alliance when placing detente in doubt." Egon Bahr, the SPD's carpenter of Ostpolitik, ridiculed candidate Reagan's drive for renewed military superiority: "Those times are over," he said. The Chancellor himself was reported to have said at the Venice summit in June 1980: "Carter is bad enough, but Reagan would be a catastrophe." And the day after the election, Theo Sommer, Schmidt's former ghost-writer, called the Reagan victory "terrible," an assessment that contrasted with Schmidt's more recent assessment that Reagan's election will strengthen America's voice in international political affairs.

The indications that these previous hostilities will soon cease are few. On the contrary, friction will develop over financial and military issues covering the fundamental political problems of different American and German roles in the Atlantic Alliance. On the one hand, America wants West Germany to contribute much more to the upkeep of American trip-wire installations in West Germany. These demands meet German counter-demands that the U.S. must first improve the general quality of its armed forces, and, in particular, "raise the level of education" in the combat ranks. A few days after the U.S. November elections Chancellor Schmidt jabbed at the dollar's weakness and the manpower shortage in the American armed forces. While rejecting demands for greater German defense spending, he declared that the freedom of the world "is not defended with paper money but by men." And ignoring America's primarily nuclear role in Europe's defense, the finance minister, Hans Matthoefer, bragged: "We can bring four million men, trained, armed, briefed, and motivated to defend their country, into position within twelve days. Whether other countries four times our size can do this remains to be seen."

The German problem, undoubtedly, will occupy center stage in the overall East-West relationship. Germany, divided after its defeat in World War II, has evolved into the Federal Republic of Germany — democratic, free, prosperous, an integrated member of the European Community and of NATO — and the German Democratic Republic, neither free nor democratic, an integrated part of the monolithic military and economic alliances of the Eastern bloc. The heart of the German and the East-West problem is West Germany's enduring commitment to reunite these two Germanies.

At the heart of the problem lies the status of Berlin, the former capital, also divided between East and West, but held hostage because of its location in the center of the German Democratic Republic. Berlin's continued freedom has always been used as a subterfuge by the Social Democrats when yet another concession had to be made to political blackmail from the East. After all, the Western allies, France, Britain, and the U.S., as legal guardians for Berlin, did nothing when the wall was built in 1961. So argued those Social Democrats like Willy Brandt and Egon Bahr, his sexton, who therefore sought the key for "peace" in Moscow. With Helmut Schmidt at the helm, detente has been given a less appeasing meaning, but the new vocabulary is not reassuring to NATO. Schmidt talks increasingly of "Germany's interest first," which includes a growing freedom of action between East and West.

Europeans speculate that Schmidt owes his success in this effort to President Carter's failure. Carter's "insensitivity has complicated relations with allies and adversaries. Not only did he start by failing to appreciate the importance of West Germany to the Western alliance, but his continuing difficulty in establishing a smooth relationship with Herr Schmidt has remained an impediment to cooperation" (*The Times*, November 3, 1980). It is no accident that the London *Sunday Times* (November 9, 1980), in its editorial on the Reagan Presidency, places the future relationship between Europe and the White House in President Reagan's and Chancellor Schmidt's hands.

During Jimmy Carter's Presidency Bonn became a more openly independent ally — with occasional impulses of appeasement toward the common adversary in the East. The softening of German commitment can be explained, in part, as a function of failing leadership in the Atlantic Alliance. This leadership can be provided only by Washington. No European could hope to substitute for the U.S. President within the Alliance, and Chancellor Schmidt certainly has shown no such ambition. Despite numerous European "reservations" about Reagan's foreign policy, despite the apprehension justified by the Europeans' recent record in defense spending, Europeans can be expected to toe the line under President Reagan. Americans cannot be surprised if Ronald Reagan's proposed foreign and defense policy has intimidated those Europeans who in the most recent past had become used to supporting and rationalizing a U.S. foreign policy of decline and to suffer under the impact of America's floundering economy.

At the start of a new Presidency Europe in general believes that America needs to restore a sound monetary policy, to balance the budget, and to bring inflation under control. This is also a European interest. American inflation has been spilling over into the rest of the Atlantic Alliance, spoiling anti-inflationary policies in European countries, and affecting defense budgets. With the right policies President Reagan might well mill

trans-Atlantic relations into an Alliance again, especially if, as he promised, Americans will not allow themselves simply to react, simply to be at the command of
world events. The "strongest of all the Greeks in ships,
infantry, cavalry, and revenue" might even make the
best of them.